Christian Healing Rediscovered

a guide to
spiritual,
mental,
physical
wholeness

Roy Lawrence

InterVarsity Press
Downers Grove
Illinois 60515

InterVarsity Press is the book-publishing division of Inter-Varsity Christian Fellowship, a student movement active on campus at hundreds of universities, colleges and schools of nursing. For information about local and regional activities, write IVCF, 233 Langdon St., Madison, WI 53703.

Distributed in Canada through InterVarsity Press, 1875 Leslie St., Unit 10, Don Mills, Ontario M3B 2M5, Canada.

All Scripture quotations, unless otherwise indicated, are from the Revised Standard Version of the Bible, copyrighted 1946, 1952, © 1971, 1973.

ISBN 0-87784-621-9

Printed in the United States of America

Library of Congress Cataloging in Publication Data
Lawrence, Roy, 1931-
    Christian healing rediscovered.
    "A combined edition of Christian healing rediscovered (1976) and Invitation to healing (1979)."
    1. Spiritual healing. 2. Lawrence, Roy, 1931-
I. Lawrence, Roy, 1931-   Invitation to healing.
II. Title.
BT732.5.L33 1980   253   80-7470
ISBN 0-87784-621-9

17	16	15	14	13	12	11	10	9	8	7	6	5	4	3	2
94	93	92	91	90	89	88	87	86	85	84	83	82	81		

Preface

It has been said that there is nothing more powerful than "an idea whose time has come." It may well be that in Britain today Christian healing is such an idea. People have been thinking and praying about it for many years, but suddenly it seems that in a new way we have "liftoff."

I have been privileged to have a small part in the development of this ministry. For instance, before writing this preface I went with three members of my congregation to visit a church in South Cheshire. In the afternoon we met their Parochial Church Council and later took part in their evening service. My aim was to share thoughts similar to those in this book with their church leaders and congregation. At the same time the friends who travelled with me spoke of their own personal experience of the ministry of healing.

One told of the spontaneous healing of a knee condition at one of our services. Another spoke of the way he had been helped to a "healing of relationships" at his work through our ministry. The third spoke of an American friend who received "healing by proxy" after prayer was offered for her at a service here in England. The vicar and council of that South Cheshire church decided on the spot that from now on they will hold their own monthly services of Christian healing.

This is not an isolated incident. It is an example of a movement in which many people are involved. They belong to all Christian denominations and all levels of churchmanship. With increasing regularity churches and chapels all over Britain are beginning to explore this ministry. After two recent TV services from my church on the theme of Christian healing, we were inundated with hundreds of letters and phone calls from interested individuals and churches. Increasingly there are invitations to broadcast, to write, to visit, to speak. More and more people want to know the sort of things we are discovering about the ministry of Christian healing.

We are not involved in this ministry because either I or any other member of my congregation lay claim to having any special "psychic gift" of healing. We do not. I believe that such gifts can and do exist and that, like any other gift, they can be offered to the Lord, but this is not what we understand by Christian healing. The essence of Christian healing is an encounter with the reality of the risen Jesus Christ in living worship. It is something which I believe every ordinary church is called to rediscover in our day.

This book is a combined edition of material from two books already circulating in England under the titles *Christian Healing Rediscovered* and *Invitation to Healing*. I hope and pray it will be a blessing to you.

Do not fear that in some way Christian healing is a substitute for the gospel. It is not. Speaking personally, I see myself as first and foremost called to be a minister of the gospel, communicating the reality of the saving power of Jesus. In my own ministry everything else will always be secondary to the gospel of salvation.

Do not fear that in some way Christian healing will take from you the right and duty to think through things, that it will obscure thoughtfulness with a fog of emotionalism. God gave us minds to think with, and I hope this book will lead to greater, not lesser, thoughtfulness.

Do not fear that Christian healing is in any way incompatible with a love of the Scriptures. We learn from the Bible about healing at many levels: the healing of body, mind and spirit, of relationships in family and society, and, most fundamentally, the healing of our relationship with God. I hope everything I have written in this book will have the effect of driving readers right back to the Bible.

Finally, do not fear the challenge which you may feel as you read these pages. In England many have read them and then felt called to "do something" about it in their own church, their own personal lives. If in some way the call of Christ to new aspects of life and ministry is to be heard here, then "faithful is he who calls." We have nothing to fear but our own fearfulness.

Roy Lawrence
Prenton, Birkenhead, England
March 10, 1980

1/A Challenge to Preach . . . and Heal

He could not move without pain.

I was a seminary student at the time. He was a church warden at a mission church where I was occasionally invited to assist at services. I had come to regard him with considerable respect. He had resigned from the firm for which he worked, on a point of principle, because he believed the company to be guilty of serious malpractice. He knew he was taking a risk and that there was a chance that his name would be blackened and that it would be hard for him to find other work, but he felt that as a Christian he had to make a stand.

To be without a job and without a reference was not easy, but there was worse to come. Soon after his resignation he became ill. The cause was difficult to trace, but he was told by his doctor that it might be some sort of virus infection. He was housebound. Pains in his back and limbs kept him in continuous discomfort. The condition did not respond to treatment. For month after month there was no improvement. His wife became increasingly worried. His own spirit sank lower and lower.

Then one day when I was visiting him, he said to me, "You know, if Jesus was here, he'd shift all this. He'd heal me." We thought about this in silence for a while and then it struck us both together: *Jesus was here.* We had his word for it. "Where two or three are gathered in my name, there am I"—and we two were gathered in his name. We soon knew what we had to do.

The next day we both spent the morning in prayer, I in the parish church and he at his home. In the afternoon I laid hands on him in the name of Christ. He started to improve almost immediately. A fortnight later he was riding his bicycle around the parish.

All this happened over twenty years ago and was my first conscious experience of Christian healing.

Oddly enough, I then went on virtually to forget about it! It had been wonderful while it happened, but afterward I found myself thinking, perhaps he would have got better at that time anyway, or perhaps it had all been psychosomatic. In any case, I was just about to start studying for a degree in theology at Oxford and this sort of experience seemed strangely out of place in the cool detachment of academic study. So I tucked it away at the back of my mind.

Many years later I was one of a carload of clergy on the way to a conference in Blackpool, and quite suddenly and casually someone said, "Have you noticed that when Jesus says, 'preach' he usually adds 'and heal'?"

It was just a chance comment but it was enough to bring the whole subject of Christian healing back into the forefront of my thoughts, and I found that I could not forget it. It was a disturbing comment, because if Jesus has given his church two equally important commands, "preach and heal," then the church has become lopsided. We preach our heads off—after a fashion—but the study and practice of healing has largely been lost over the centuries.

I was due to go back to Oxford for a half-term's refresher course and decided to spend part of the time looking at what the Bible has to say about healing. There I rediscovered certain basic truths which tend to be forgotten.

Healing is a primary biblical topic. In fact it is no exaggeration to say that *the Bible is a book about healing.* Its concern is the healing of the total person (body, mind and spirit), the healing of relationships, the healing of society, the healing of the nations.

"Bless the LORD, O my soul," says the psalmist, "and forget not all his benefits, who forgives all your iniquity, who *heals all your diseases*" (Ps. 103:2-3). God's essential nature is that of a healer. One of his titles is "the LORD, your healer" (Ex. 15:26). The biblical philosophy of life, if accepted, increases health. The book of Proverbs puts it quaintly but concisely, "Fear the LORD, and depart from evil. It shall be health to thy navel, and marrow to thy bones" (Prov. 3:7-8 KJV).

It followed that since Jesus came into the world to do the will of God (Jn. 6:38), healing was the will and the work of Jesus. He "saw a great throng; and he had compassion on them, and healed their sick" (Mt. 14:14). Along with the mass healings there were many instances of individual healings—blindness (Mt. 9:27-31), deafness (Mk. 7:31-35), lameness (Mt. 11:4-5), paralysis (Mt. 8:5-13), fever (Mt. 8:14-15), skin conditions (Mt. 8:1-3) and so on.

Also, Jesus made it plain that it was his will to continue his healing ministry through his church. My colleague in the car on the way to Blackpool was right. Christ's dual commission was "preach *and heal*" (Lk. 9:1-2, 6; 10:1,9). The early disciples were obedient and effective in the ministry of healing. There were mass healings (Acts 5:16) and individual healings (Acts 3:1-16; 9:32-43; 14:8-10; 28:8).

Jesus saw healing as a sign and an element in the coming

of the kingdom of God (Lk. 10:9). Isaiah had seen it in the same way centuries earlier (Is. 35:4-6).

James spelled out the practicalities for a Christian congregation. "Is any among you sick? Let him call for the elders of the church, and let them pray over him, anointing him with oil in the name of the Lord; and the prayer of faith will save the sick man, and the Lord will raise him up; and if he has committed sins, he will be forgiven. Therefore confess your sins to one another, and pray for one another, *that you may be healed*" (Jas. 5:14-16).

But what of ourselves? Most clergy, I would guess, could tell of isolated incidents in which they have prayed with the sick and perhaps laid on hands in the name of Christ, and there have been remarkable occasions of healing.

As I thought of it for myself, the incident of the healing of the church warden came back into my mind and I remembered that after my ordination there were other similar incidents, not all that many, perhaps one every couple of years. Other clergy with whom I talked described much the same situation. Christian healing was an actuality for us—but an occasional one. It tended to be on the periphery of our thought and practice. We tended to think of it as an extra, and a rather surprising one.

This clearly is not good enough. It is not the sort of balance which Jesus had in mind when he envisaged the ministry of his disciples. "Preach and heal" does not mean two sermons every Sunday and a healing perhaps every other year. He did not lead us to expect a diminution in the availability of healing power. The disciples were to do more, not less, than Jesus did (Jn. 14:12). Was he perhaps just thinking of the spread of the message of salvation when he told them this? Was he excluding the ministry of healing? Not at all. For salvation and healing are inseparably interrelated in the Bible. In fact in our English New Testament "save" and "heal" often translate the same Greek word. *Sōzō* and *diasōzō* mean both "save" (ninety four times in the New Testament) and "heal" (sixteen times in the New Testament).

As my refresher course at Oxford progressed, I could see all this with increasing clarity.

The question was, what was I going to do about it when the time came for me to return to my parish?

2/Toward a Service of Healing

There were various options open to me when I returned from the half-term refresher course at Oxford to my parish of St. George's, Hyde. I could have said nothing to anybody but quietly intensified the element of healing in my personal pastoral ministry. This really did not seem sufficient. Or I could have gathered a like-minded group and started a small midweek service of prayer for healing. This did not seem sufficient either. If healing is the basic life and work of the whole church, it is not sufficient to tuck it away in a corner. I felt a strong leading to introduce the theme of Christian healing into the mainstream of the worship of my church at a regular Sunday service.

There were difficulties, of course. There was my ignorance, which was vast. There were my doubts which had to be acknowledged and faced. "How do I know it really works? Suppose my experiences so far have all been coincidences?" There were my fears. "Supposing it all goes wrong? What will be left of my faith? Will I look a fool? Is there a chance I might actually harm people by giving them false hope?"

But amid the mental turmoil there was at any rate one absolute certainty. I knew without doubt that Christian healing is a topic of such importance and such biblical centrality that it is vital for the church to be looking at it hard and straight, researching into it, bringing thought, prayer, Bible study and the light of historical and personal experience to bear upon an honest serious investigation till we know both the facts of the matter and the nature of God's call to us.

Normally we do not do this—or so it seems to me. We take up what appears to be basically a hypocritical position. On the one hand we preach about the healing miracles as though they did happen. On the other hand we act as though they did not happen. We even pray as though they did not happen, introducing the words "if it be thy will" as a sort of safety clause in prayer for healing. This type of doublethink is neither honest nor effective. If we know that Christian healing is a fundamentally important matter but we are not sure where faith and fact should be leading us, the honest thing is to say so and to start looking and learning.

So having talked it over with the Parochial Church Council, what we did was to start a monthly service of "Investigation into Christian Healing." It took place on the first Sunday of the month at 6:30 P.M. Basically it was the Anglican service of Evensong, but there were one or two differences. In the intercessions we prayed by name for sick folk known to us. At first the list was fairly short but quickly, as the practice became known, the list became longer. We used the same list of names for intercession week by week at a Thursday midmorning Communion service, and the list was left hanging on the wall at the back of the church in the hope that people would come in and use it for private prayer.

The sermon at an "Investigation into Christian Healing" was an examination of some aspect of healing. During the first year we looked in broad terms at the place of healing in the life and teaching of Jesus, at its place in the teaching of the Bible as a whole, at the actual historical experience of the church and at personal experiences, both my own and those shared with me by other people. We tried both to use our powers of reason and to be sensitive to the guiding of the Holy Spirit. From the second year onward we began to go chapter by chapter through Luke's Gospel, paying particular attention to the theme of healing as it arose, finding that it always did arise in one way or another. We bought copies of Luke's Gospel from the British and Foreign Bible Society. These were handed to members of the congregation as they entered church and collected before they left so that all could have the text before them as the sermon was preached.

Following the sermon a laying on of hands in the name of Christ was made available to anyone wishing to receive it. Anyone was free to come to the communion rail during the singing of the hymn after the sermon. The invitation was always put in the widest terms, "You are welcome to receive a laying on of hands and a prayer in the name of Christ if you wish to do so for any reason at all. Perhaps you have been ill in some way and have a need for physical healing. Perhaps you are feeling anxious or depressed or have a need for mental healing. Perhaps some temptation is hard to cope with and you are conscious of the need for spiritual healing. Or, if you wish, you may come forward just as an act of commitment, a prayer for spiritual deepening. Or perhaps you want to come forward as an act of prayer for someone else whom you know to be in need of healing. The touch of Christ is desirable for its own sake, quite apart from any by-products it may bring. So whatever your reasons for coming forward you are welcome."

Two of us were behind the communion rail, a clergyman and a layman. First we administered a laying on of hands to each other with the prayer, "May the healing power of the Holy Spirit be in you." Then we waited for any who wished to come forward, ready to offer the same prayer and the same touch. Out of a congregation of about a hundred, thirty or forty came forward on the first occasion to kneel at the communion rail. The number was about the same at each of the healing services during the first eighteen months. As there were three clergy on the staff and a fair number of suitable laymen and women, we were able to vary the ministrants month by month.

The words of the prayer, "May the healing power of the Holy Spirit be in you," were said in unison by the two ministrants. The congregation stood for the singing of the hymn and then knelt in silence while the laying on of hands was completed. Month by month we studied and prayed and laid on hands and waited to see what would happen.

The first thing we noticed was that there was a steady and perceptible improvement in the quality of the worship. St. George's, Hyde, is a "chatty" church. Before and after services there is a buzz of conversation. It was so well entrenched as a habit, that short of sticking tape over the congregation's lips as they entered I could see no way of stopping it! However before a service of healing the church was noticeably quieter and sometimes even absolutely quiet. During the service there was often an atmosphere of extraordinary spiritual concentration. This had nothing to do with emotionalism. Our services of healing have always been unemotional, more akin to a Communion service than to an evangelistic rally. However, having said that, the second noticeable feature of these services was the opportunity which they presented for Christian challenge. Healing and the proclamation of the gospel got together naturally and, I would say, inevitably. Christian healing is a ministry to the whole man. It cannot be divorced from the gentle exposition of the saving power of Christ.

The odd thing was that during the first eighteen months of our services of healing the one thing which we did not see was physical healing. We looked for it and longed for it—overmuch as we later came to think—but we did not see it. In fact it seemed that there was more than our normal ration of sickness in the church during these eighteen months. The church officers and I also became increasingly aware of some of the problems and difficulties associated with Christian healing.

At this stage we made an important decision. We acknowledged our need for help. We knew enough of the problems and the issues. We needed the help and guidance of someone who not only knew the problems but also knew some of the answers and had tested these answers on the anvil of his own experience.

3/A Flow
of Healing

We were fortunate in finding exactly the help we needed. It came to us through the ministry of George Bennett, a remarkable man with a remarkable mission.

George Bennett was ordained in the Church of England back in 1935. Brought up in a medical family he had begun to study medicine at Birmingham University when he experienced a conversion from agnosticism to Christianity and was called to the ministry. During the earlier part of his ministry he was in turn a curate, a vicar, a hospital chaplain, an industrial chaplain and a cathedral canon. But his main work was to begin in 1958 when he took charge of a center at Crowhurst in Sussex which devoted itself to Christian healing. This center has come to be regarded with widespread respect. It has been visited by and registered with the Medical Officer of Health and listed in the King Edward's Hospital Directory. Hundreds of patients have passed through and benefited from it. The story of this center is told by George Bennett in his book *Miracle at Crowhurst* which, along with the companion volume *The Heart of Healing,* has itself exercised a ministry of healing among readers.

For many years George Bennett made himself free to answer invitations to address groups, lead conferences and conduct missions here and overseas, and travel to the far side of the world healing and teaching. I met him for the first time when BBC Radio Manchester sent me to conduct a brief interview with him for a religious magazine program. The producer and I were both very impressed with him on this occasion. Simplicity, balance and holiness shone through the interview. So it was arranged that on Sunday, June 23, 1974 George Bennett would speak at our evening service, expounding the church's healing role in society, on Monday evening he would answer "Any Questions," and on Tuesday evening he would conduct a service of Christian healing. It was also arranged that the visit would include a half-hour broadcast on Radio Manchester and a day conference for clergy of the diocese of Chester.

We had six months to prepare for the mission. We wrote to local clergy, doctors, nurses, physiotherapists, probation officers, social service workers and others to tell them what was happening and, where necessary, to present the case for a spiritual dimension in healing. We also distributed circulars to a thousand homes.

Two very encouraging things happened in the weeks immediately before the mission. Three local churches, two Anglican and one Free Church, canceled their own evening services on Sunday, June 23 so that their clergy and congregations could participate fully in the mission. Other churches indicated their willingness to participate on Monday and Tuesday evenings. This, in a neighborhood where traditionally there has been a certain competitiveness between the churches, was itself a work of healing. Also for the first time since our healing services started, there began to be reports of healing. Granada Television asked for permission to televise part of the healing service and after some hesitation while we prayed and thought about it, it seemed right to agree.

So the mission began and very memorable it proved. It was memorable for the quality of worship. The atmosphere of prayer was strong and full of power, though as in the case of our own "Investigation into Christian Healing" services there was no undue emotionalism. The mission was memorable for the cutting of denominational differences down to size. Since then there has been a marked improvement in interdenominational and interchurch relationships in Hyde. The mission was certainly a major factor in this. The mission was memorable also for the record number of questions on Monday evening, exceeding every other place George had visited including his American visits. It was memorable for the numbers attending—800 on Tuesday with over 700 receiving a laying on of hands from George Bennett and a team of six local clergy. The half-hour program on BBC Radio Manchester was also memorable. Tape recordings of it have been used subsequently to stimulate many church groups. And the conference for clergy of the diocese of Chester was a great occasion, making an impact on many a ministry.

Tuesday evening was a night to remember. We knew the TV crew quite well by then. The producer, director and researcher attended church on all three nights, though the job itself did not require them to do so. We had some misgivings about their presence. The church was quite cluttered with extra lights and TV equipment. We knew that there would be people in church for whom the service would mean a great deal, people whose needs were great and whose hopes were great. It would have been very sad if they were to be distracted or if the service were to be turned into some sort of a show. We need not have worried. The TV crew said that they had never been so ignored in their lives!

We sang a selection of hymns. I led an extemporaneous prayer, though that is not my normal custom. George Bennett spoke briefly. Then the people came forward by the hundred to receive the laying on of hands in the name of Christ. Most did not receive the touch of George Bennett. He was flanked by three clergy on each side. So there were fourteen hands and only two were George's. But he made it quite clear that this was irrelevant, that it was not the touch of Bennett but the touch of Christ which heals and that the touch of Christ is conveyed by the body of Christ, the church.

Afterward there was a TV interview at the vicarage involving George Bennett and the TV interviewer Mike Scott. The TV crew stayed on for hours after their job was finished, talking, asking questions, drinking endless cups of coffee. The producer said that for the first time that evening he had seen what worship was actually for. He had seen the point of hymns, the point of prayer, the point of a Christian congregation. I missed most of it because in the middle of it all a man who was feeling suicidal turned up for counseling. But in due course he went home, and the TV people went away and next day George Bennett went home. And it was over. Or was it?

It was almost as though arranging the Mission of Teaching and Healing turned on a tap. The healings started to flow—physical, mental and spiritual in their effect.

They started before the actual mission. For instance a man who had been off work for months with high blood pressure found that following a laying on of hands his blood pressure became absolutely normal. Beforehand, he had to take tablets to combat the high blood pressure. Afterward, not only did he no longer need the tablets, they actually made him feel ill. Without them he was normal. There was nothing to prove it had anything to do with Christian healing. It could have been a coincidence. But if so, it was the first of many such "coincidences."

I was asked to see a housewife who was suffering from a phobic condition. She was in a sorry state, afraid to leave the house, afraid to answer the door, afraid even to answer the telephone. We talked for over an hour. We prayed together and I administered a laying on of hands in the name of Christ. Within minutes the condition began to lift. Next day she felt normal. She was able to go out into the town center and do the family shopping without ill effect. The phobia did not return.

One of the congregation had a heart incident. Her doctor told her that she should give up smoking, but when I visited her she said that she was incapable of doing so. She said she was a slave to cigarettes. As she lay in bed, there was an open packet of cigarettes on the bedside table. She said she just had to have it there within easy reach. I said to her, "Let's see what the Lord can do about it." There and then we prayed together, not specifically about the cigarettes, but about the goodness and power and love of Christ. In his name I administered a laying on of hands. A fortnight later I met her leaning on her gate. "You'll never believe it," she said. "I haven't had a single cigarette since you visited me. I just haven't wanted to." Since then she has not smoked. The urge has gone.

With the mission came other reports of healing. For instance, the mother-in-law of a local fish and chips shop proprietor had suffered for ten years with swollen, painful legs. She found it difficult to walk and had to be assisted into church at the mission service of healing. She was brought forward for a laying on of hands. The hands were not those of George Bennett, but belonged to a young clergyman who was feeling rather depressed and inadequate in the ministry. It was a characteristic gesture of God that this young clergyman's hands were used in the first instance of healing reported in connection with the mission. As the woman returned to her seat, she said to her son-in-law, "All the pain has gone." By the time she arrived back home her legs not only felt normal, they looked normal. Six months later I met her in the street and hardly recognized her. She looked ten years younger. Before, she could hardly walk. Now she could run! She could dance!

That particular family did rather well from the mission. The chip shop proprietor's wife had for some time suffered from back pains. She told me that tests had revealed a urinary infection. After the service of healing the back pains ceased and further tests showed that there was now nothing amiss.

A man with an acute depression wrote to me before the mission. He wondered whether he could find help because life was hardly worth living. A fortnight later he telephoned to say that his condition had improved remarkably. He had been able to stop all his tablets except for a couple of sleeping pills. He felt and sounded a new man.

There was no mistaking the gladness and peace on the faces of dozens of people who talked with me about the personal meaning of the mission for them. They spoke of burdens being lifted, of new dimensions of living and of new glimpses of the reality and meaning of Christ. One elderly parishioner said it was like starting life all over again!

I heard too of a healing over a year before: an unpleasant and recurrent skin condition cleared completely after a period of counseling and laying on of hands. If only we could have heard of this earlier. It happened in the middle of the period when there seemed to be no signs of physical healing anywhere and we were soldiering on with our services of "Investigation into Christian Healing" in spite of an apparent lack of results. It would have been such an encouragement to have known about it at the time.

However, in a strange way, though we were now hearing of these and other healings, they were less important to us than they would have been before. For we were now learning more clearly the difference between Christian healing and the mere working of cures. Christian healing is concerned not so much with cures as with wholeness; with that harmony with God which helps a person to be more of a person than he was before, spiritually, mentally, physically. Christian healing lifts up the risen Christ not as a means to an end but as an end in itself. We all need healing. We all need Christ. In a Christian healing service we seek the touch of Christ upon our lives, simply because Christ is infinitely desirable. Cures, lovely though they are, are just by-products.

Cures are not the only by-products of a venture in Christian healing. The discernible deepening in the quality of worship and the sharpened capacity for evangelism have already been mentioned. They continued to develop. So too did the increasing sense of Christian unity. For example a local nonconformist church decided that once a quarter it would close its own evening service so that minister and congregation could be one with the people of St. George's in our service of healing. This joint service was always a happy and worthwhile occasion to which I looked forward. It was good also to receive letters of encouragement and support from people of all denominations—a Baptist minister in Kent, a doctor who has become a minister, a retired sea captain, a Cornish vicar, a Roman Catholic nun in a French convent who prayed for the healing ministry of St. George's, Hyde, on the first Sunday of each month at 6:30 P.M. Everywhere it seemed there were new friends, new partners in healing.

We seemed to have been given a sharpened awareness of the basic issues of the faith. It was, for instance, a real pleasure to be at the meeting of the Parochial Church Council which followed the mission. Members spoke of the meaning which the mission had held for them personally. Two members of the congregation have now offered themselves for the ministry, an event unheard of in the life of that church. And surprisingly we found that groups of the congregation were invited to talk to other churches and other groups to share our experience of Christian healing and other discoveries which we are making about the meaning of being a responsible member of a responsible church. We found that in God's economy nothing was wasted. We learned much during the first eighteen months investigating Christian healing and the parish has been able to use it all.

There is another by-product of involvement in healing which should be mentioned. I hesitate to write about it because it was strange and painful, and I would prefer to forget it. But it should be included both for the sake of completeness and in case others have to face it. Some weeks after the mission, even though we were surrounded by lovely and encouraging events, a number of our church leaders underwent a period of darkness and oppression. It happened simultaneously to all three clergy, to the church wardens and to the church secretary. It was a horrible thing, full of morbid fancies and the temptation to despair.

Previously I had assumed that only the attractive could tempt, but it is not so. Strangely enough, my own experience of this oppression took place actually during a holiday period. All around me were scenes of beauty. There was opportunity for leisure and enjoyment. Yet through it all there was something horrid, hard to describe, a sort of weight of darkness, pressing down. It was a relief to find that others were going through it too. With mutual support and prayer it passed. It has been suggested to us that we were under some sort of attack—and certainly this is just what it felt like.

As we gathered our wits after this strange experience, we discovered a renewed sense of expectancy. I felt able to rename our service on the first Sunday of the month. Till then it had been an "Investigation into Christian Healing." Now we felt able to call it a "Rediscovery of Christian Healing." Our ignorance was still great. It *is* still great. But in one way or another our experience had led us to the point where we now knew that there is a deep reality of healing to be rediscovered if we are faithful to our Lord.

4/A New Start

A little over a year later, in October 1975, my family and I moved to the parish of Prenton, on the outskirts of Birkenhead. Prenton is a mixed area, ranging from public housing at the perimeter to some quite large homes at the center. There are shops, schools and sports clubs, including Tranmere Rovers Football Club. All of these are built on and around a little hill. At the top of the hill stands St. Stephen's Church, with the church hall and the vicarage next to it, and halfway down the hill there is the daughter church, St. Alban's, with a youth center and a curacy house next door.

It is a busy, varied parish, full of interesting possibilities and opportunities. The church folk are kindly, unobtrusive people who would not consider themselves remarkable in any way. The congregations have not for some time

been remarkable for their size. And the people in the congregations are predominantly quiet and shy, in no way
remarkable for their powers of evangelism. But there is one
sense at least in which I believe they are truly remarkable.
For the church people of Prenton, serving the Lord seems
automatically to involve serving the community. They find
it natural to respond in his name to the needs of those
around them.

Month by month, literally hundreds of hours are spent
by the church folk of Prenton running clubs for the elderly,
play groups for toddlers, a youth center, a sheltered housing scheme and many other caring activities. There are so
many examples of this which come to mind as I write: the
annual holiday for the elderly run by one of our ladies (herself a pensioner), the monthly tea party for the elderly, the
marathon turkey-and-trimmings dinner provided by pa-
rishioners for seventy or more lonely people on Christmas
day, the church couple who have fostered forty-eight children over the years and yet have still found time for the
wife to run a play group and the husband to help at the
youth center.

I can report this without inhibition because I am in no
way responsible for it. This is the way in which I found the
parish. If credit is due to the clergy for it, it must go to my
predecessors.

When a parish has an atmosphere of community care
and concern, there are many reasons to thank God for it.
One of the good things about it is that it is a natural atmosphere for a ministry of healing. Without love there can be
no Christian healing. For Jesus, loving and healing were
inseparably intertwined, and the church which has begun
to love in his name has, whether it knows it or not, already
begun to do his work of healing.

So I found that I was able to begin services of Christian
healing in Prenton in an unself-conscious and almost
casual fashion. The church officers knew that soon after my
arrival these services would begin. I had made this clear

before accepting the post. But apart from that there was no
fanfare of trumpets before the first Christian healing service. One evening it just happened. It seemed right to use
the sermon to speak about the basic facts of Christian healing and to tell something of the story of this ministry in my
former parish. At the end of the sermon I said that our
Church Army Captain and I would be standing behind the
communion rail during the hymn that followed and that if
anyone wished to come to us we would be ready and will-
ing to administer a laying on of hands in the name of our
Lord. And forward they came—about twenty out of a small
congregation of thirty or forty. The services of healing had
started.

Before long a format had evolved for these services. It
was similar to, though not identical with, the format of the
services of healing in Hyde. We started with a shortened
form of Series Two Evensong, reading one lesson only and
using only one canticle. After trying various canticles the
one we came to settle for was the little-known *Salvator
Mundi* which contains so many of the basic underlying
truths of Christian healing.

O Saviour of the world, the Son Lord Jesus:
Stir up thy strength and help us, we humbly beseech thee.
By thy cross and precious blood thou hast redeemed us:
Save us and help us, we humbly beseech thee.
Thou didst save thy disciples when ready to perish:
Hear us and save us, we humbly beseech thee.
Let the pitifulness of thy great mercy:
Loose us from our sins, we humbly beseech thee.
Make it appear that thou art our Saviour and mighty
   Deliverer:
O save us that we may praise thee, we humbly beseech thee.
Draw near according to thy promise from the throne of
   thy glory:
Look down and hear our crying, we humbly beseech thee.
Come again and dwell with us, O Lord Christ Jesus:
Abide with us for ever, we humbly beseech thee.

And when thou shalt appear with power and great glory:
May we be made like unto thee in thy glorious kingdom.
Thanks be to thee, O Lord.
Alleluia! Amen.

The sermon, as in Hyde, soon came to consist of a Bible study, moving chapter by chapter through Luke's Gospel, paying particular attention to the theme of healing as it arose—and finding that it always did arise in one way or another. Copies of Luke's Gospel were handed to members of the congregation as they entered church and collected before they left, so that all could have the text before them as the sermon was preached. The same passage was read as the lesson earlier in the service.

During the hymn after the sermon a laying on of hands in the name of Christ was made available to anyone wishing to receive it. Anyone was free to come to the communion rail. The invitation was put in much the same way as had become customary at Hyde:

You are welcome to receive a laying on of hands and a prayer in the name of Christ if you wish to do so for any reason at all. Perhaps you have been ill in some way and have a need for physical healing. Perhaps you are feeling anxious or depressed and have a need for mental healing. Perhaps some temptation is hard to cope with and you are conscious of the need for spiritual healing. Or, if you wish, you may come forward just as an act of commitment, a prayer for spiritual deepening, a symbol of your availability to our Lord. Or perhaps you want to come forward as an act of prayer for someone else, whom you know to be in need of healing. Or perhaps you want to come forward simply because the touch of Christ is desirable for its own sake, quite apart from any by-products it may bring. Whatever your reasons for coming forward, you are welcome.

Initially, two of us were behind the communion rail. Then, at subsequent services, as the number coming forward grew from twenty to thirty, forty, fifty and sixty, we increased the number of ministrants to two teams of two.

First we administered a laying on of hands to each other with the prayer, "May the healing power of the Holy Spirit be in you," said in unison; then, two by two, we offered the same prayer and the same touch to those who came forward from the congregation.

I was fortunate that the Church Army Captain who was working in the parish before my arrival saw the point of Christian healing and agreed fully with this ministry. Soon we were joined by a curate who was also happy to involve himself in this ministry of healing. The lay readers also agreed to participate. So did a growing number of our church officers. As in Hyde, I was always happy to see a clergyman and a layman administering the laying on of hands together—the touch of Christ given by the body of Christ.

The prayers of intercession followed the laying on of hands. As the hymn finished, the congregation knelt for silent individual prayer, and as the laying on of hands finished, the silent individual prayer merged into a period of corporate prayer. Then the worship ended with a hymn of praise and a blessing.

Right from the start, this service was received with thoughtfulness and graciousness in the parish. Before long it was received with positive gratefulness. I realize this does not always happen when a service of healing is introduced into the worship of a church. For instance, two parishes come to mind where the vicars have experienced difficulty in introducing a ministry of healing. In one, the Parochial Church Council has split into two factions, a pro-charismatic and an anticharismatic group, and the ministry of healing has become a sort of football to be kicked between the two. In another a group of local doctors have misunderstood the purpose of the ministry of Christian healing and have reacted to the vicar with open hostility.

There have been no such traumas during the first few years of this ministry in Prenton. Just before writing this paragraph I have been out to administer a laying on of hands in the name of Christ to a local doctor, who is ill at present and who has received a ministry of Christian healing with gratitude and humility. Other local doctors have discussed the subject with me with sympathy and understanding. The people of the church also have shown a spirit of openness which in many cases has now developed into a spirit of awareness and commitment.

Why have things worked out in this way in Prenton? Several factors seem to be involved.

I have already mentioned the "casual" approach which now seems to be the best method of introduction. Truth is a self-validating concept. It needs no fanfare of trumpets. If there are tangible initial results, they will provide more than enough of a fanfare themselves. If there are not, then any previous fanfare would be something of an embarrassment.

The spirit of kindliness and community concern which I found already existent in Prenton has already been mentioned. This is important. Christian healing does not happen in a vacuum. It can be actively impeded by undercurrents of bitterness and mistrust in the life of a church. But it is nurtured and fostered by a spirit of simple practical Christian love.

There are other considerations also. I suppose there was a good deal more certainty on my part in my introduction of the ministry of healing at Prenton than there had been at Hyde. The only certainty I had in the early days at Hyde was that Christian healing is a topic of such importance that our church should investigate the subject for ourselves. We were especially concerned to know the nature of God's call to us. The service was an investigation, a groping toward a light which was not discerned clearly or constantly. That was the way it had to be, because we have to be honest in our approach to Christian healing or we shall damage ourselves and the Christian cause. Wishful thinking must never be a substitute for truth and experience.

However, by the time I brought this ministry to Prenton, I knew a little more of the truth and had a certain degree of experience on which to draw. Mind you, I am still very much a beginner. All that I can claim is that perhaps I have moved out of the kindergarten and into first grade in the school of Christian healing. Still, even that degree of progress brings with it an instinctive increase in authority.

I was fortunate, too, in that back in the 1940s, while I was still a schoolboy, a previous vicar of Prenton had been concerned for the ministry of healing. There is still talk of a "miracle cure" which took place in his day. Memories of his ministry meant that Christian healing was not regarded as completely newfangled or unknown.

Also it was certainly a help that, in the early days of Christian healing services at Prenton, there were some lovely instances of healing.

One such instance concerned one of our church wardens, a local dentist, who fell down a flight of stairs and broke five ribs. He was admitted to the hospital but went on to develop double virus pneumonia. His condition deteriorated and there were fears for his life. He lay in bed with a raging temperature, absolutely soaking with great drops of sweat which you could actually see exuding from his skin.

I went to the hospital. We prayed together and I administered a laying on of hands in the Lord's name. It was like touching someone who had come straight out of a bath. I needed a towel to dry my hands.

Soon afterward while I was still sitting by his bed, a nurse came with a thermometer for a routine temperature check. She took his temperature and then went for a second thermometer. "This one must be broken," she explained, "it says his temperature's normal, and it can't be." However, it *was* normal! The second thermometer confirmed it—and a steady recovery followed.

Of course, there is no way of "proving" that the prayers

and the laying on of hands had anything to do with that recovery, but our warden had no doubts about it, and subsequently he asked if he might speak to the congregation at one of our healing services. He is a shy man, not a natural talker and certainly not one to wear his heart on his sleeve. It was very moving indeed to hear him speak simply and sincerely of his experience of the touch of Christ and of his certainty that this touch had brought peace and healing where before there was turbulence and danger.

So with this help and with the cooperation and good will of my colleagues and the other church officers, the service of Christian healing became a regular and valued part of the life of the church in Prenton.

5/Healing Prayer

In the early days of the healing ministry at Hyde I used to follow the practice of reading out a long list of names of people who were sick or in some sort of trouble, and sometimes I would add a description of whatever was wrong with them: "Today our prayers are asked for Eliza Smith who has shingles, John Brown with lung cancer, little Julie Robinson whose mother has just died, George Thompson whose arthritis seems to be getting worse, Emily Jones now confined to a wheelchair with multiple sclerosis, Wally Wilkinson who has had a heart attack, Brenda Moody in the hospital after a nervous breakdown . . ." and so on, for perhaps thirty, forty or fifty names. The object, of course, was to bring to them the healing power of Christ, channeled by prayer, and there were not a few occasions when healing did, in fact, follow.

However, there is a risk in this method of prayer. The risk is that instead of lifting the sufferers whose names we mention into the positive presence of Christ, our own minds will be filled with thoughts of their sickness and suffering and we shall end up by worrying about the destructive power of disease rather than meditating on the healing power of Christ. People could go away depressed by this sort of "prayer," rather than uplifted by it. This was brought to my notice when attendance at the midweek Communion service where the list of the sick was read dropped markedly for a while, because people said it made them feel so miserable.

At Hyde we found a partial solution in reading a list of names only, without any mention of symptoms or ailments, but even this could produce a rather negative effect. However, at Prenton we have, I believe, found a better way. The parish tradition is to place the prayers after the sermon and not before it, as in most churches. So the prayers and not the sermon are the climax of the service. This has proved particularly fitting in our service of Christian healing. In the sermon we catch a glimpse of the healing Christ, in the laying on of hands we feel his healing touch, and in the prayers we enjoy his presence and lift into that presence the needs of the world. We still have scores of individual requests for prayer. These we write in an intercession book.

Of course God knows the names that are written in this book and the people to whom those names belong and the needs and problems of all those people. He knows all this much more exactly than we do. He also knows those people whose names should be in the book but have been left out because of some fault of ours or because of our ignorance. What we now do is first to recollect the presence of the risen, living, healing Christ, and then without reading a list of individual names and ailments we offer the book and its contents to God and offer our prayers as the channels of this power, love and peace. We pray that his holy and healing will may be done in body, mind and spirit, in life and in circumstance, for all those whose names are written or should be written in our book of intercession, and we thank God that we can know as we pray that his healing power is active in the world. This is a positive experience for those who are praying and good results are reported to us among those for whom we pray.

By a strange "coincidence" just as I have written the last sentence, two such results have been reported to me. The Lord has an impeccable sense of timing! First came a telephone report of an improvement in a nervous condition from a member of a nearby church, for whom we have been praying for some months. And then hard on the heels of this came a report from a member of St. Alban's, our daughter church, about a relative in America who has been suffering from double vision. After inclusion on our prayer list, the condition cleared almost immediately.

News like this comes to us with increasing frequency. When we hear it we feel a tremendous sense of privilege. When a church embarks upon a serious ministry of Christian healing it seems that this ministry reaches out not just to people who are present in church but to people who have never attended our services and who may live many miles away.

A lady comes to mind—let's call her Agatha—who phoned me a year ago from her home in North Wales. She was suffering from dangerously high blood pressure. No treatment seemed to bring it down. Her doctor was worried. She was worried, and the more she worried the worse her condition became. Then she heard of our healing ministry and telephoned to tell me about her high blood pressure and to ask for prayer. I promised to include her on our intercession list. Three months later she phoned to say that her condition was no longer critical. The pills she was taking seemed at last to be working. In a further three months she phoned again to say that the improvement had continued and that the medical treatment had been reduced.

So far this chapter has dealt with general principles. I want to turn now to something more specific and detailed —a method of healing prayer which we use from time to time at our Christian healing service, and which can also be used privately. I call it "the ring of peace." Various people have told me that they find it an effective method of prayer. Try it and see for yourself.

1. Begin by recollecting the presence of Christ. If you are praying within a group, your group has the promise of Jesus: "Where two or three are gathered in my name, there am I in the midst" (Mt. 18:20). If you are in private prayer, he is still with you. You have his word: "I am with you always, to the close of the age" (Mt. 28:20).

2. So there you are, you and Jesus. What sort of experience is it to be in his presence? He has not changed; he "is the same yesterday and today and for ever" (Heb. 13:8). He is the same Jesus who went about "preaching the gospel of the kingdom and healing every disease and every infirmity among the people" (Mt. 4:23). He is the same Jesus who promised his disciples, "Peace I leave with you; my peace I give to you" (Jn. 14:27). If we are available to him, open to him as Savior and Lord, not fighting him but prepared for him to have his way with us, then we are within the healing peace of God which Jesus came to bring to us.

3. There is a common error concerning the peace of God. We tend to think of it as something rather precarious which we have to strive hard to hold and keep or else it will slip away, whereas the biblical picture is precisely the opposite. "The peace of God, which passes all understanding, will keep your hearts and your minds in Christ Jesus" (Phil. 4:7). We do not keep the peace of God. The peace of God keeps us. So the mental picture which I suggest for this meditation is that of yourself surrounded by the ring of God's peace. There is no need to strive. Just rest in the knowledge that it is so.

4. There is another common error which thinks of the

peace of God as a weak and passive concept. But the peace
of God is no mere absence of turmoil. It is strong and active
and vibrant with life. It must be so because it is an attribute
of God himself. A common title of God in the New Testament is "the God of peace." The peace of God is one with
the power of God, and the love of God, and the joy of God.
To be within God's ring of peace is to be in contact with
God's power and love and joy. It is a place of creativity, a
place of healing.

5. So there is no need to do anything. Just "let go" before the Lord. Acknowledge his peace. Enjoy his peace. Let
his peace flow round you. Let his peace flow into you—
warm, strong and life-giving. There is no hurry. You can
rest in this place of healing as long as you choose to do so.
You can actually feel the peace of God entering into every
part of your mind, every part of your body, the very depths
of your spirit. You can know that sin and tension and sickness must retreat before it.

6. When the time is right, bring others into the ring of
peace. Picture your family within the ring of peace. Lift up
each member into that peace. Thank God that it is his will
that your home should be a place of his peace and that
peace should undergird all the relationships of family life,
and as you thank God, offer your prayer as the instrument
and vehicle of his will. Then bring into the ring of peace
any known to you who are ill or in trouble. In each case do
not concentrate on the illness or the trouble. Think of each
one as a person created and loved by God, a person for
whom God's will is wholeness. Let your prayer reinforce
God's will as you picture yourself and the one for whom
you are praying within the ring of peace. Again do not
strive or worry or tense up. Let God's own peace do God's
own work.

7. In our service of healing, we imagine the ring of peace
growing larger and larger. After picturing our individual
selves within the ring of God's peace, we encircle the
whole congregation, all of us in church—our families too—

with that same ring of peace. We thank God for each other. We thank God for himself in our midst. We thank God that his presence and his peace are not passive, but actively at work in that moment, full of purpose and power. Then we bring within the ring of peace all those for whom we have been asked to pray, all those whose names are, or should be, in our intercession book. We read no list of names and ailments, but simply align our prayers with God's holy and healing will, offering ourselves as channels of that will for peace and wholeness. As a symbol of this prayer, I usually lift and hold the intercession book as we pray. Then we picture the ring of peace around our neighborhood, then around our country, then encircling our world, and finally surrounding the whole universe known and unknown. "Thy holy and healing will be done," we pray, and we thank God that we can offer this prayer with confidence. The will of the almighty and eternal God must ultimately triumph, his peace must prevail, his kingdom will come— because he is God. So these are strong prayers, not weak prayers. We can offer them not with anxiety but with calm expectancy.

There are many methods of healing prayer. This is only one. May I ask that you put this book down at the end of this chapter and rest awhile within the ring of peace yourself, going through the stages one by one without hurrying?

There have been a number of occasions when I have been grateful to do this myself. Once I had to attend a BBC Morning Service Course at the Churches' TV and Radio Centre at Bushey, near Watford. It was clearly going to be an exacting course, and I could learn a great deal from it. The trouble was that I had just started with what promised to be a nasty cold. My nose was blocked, my throat was sore and by any normal prognosis things would get worse. I decided that I had to put the journey along the highway from Birkenhead to Bushey to good use by spending that time in healing prayer.

So for three hours or so I alternated the ring of peace sequence of prayer with a meditation on the work of the Holy Spirit, which will be described later in this book. This improved my driving, if anything, because one's mind is certainly not less clear or less efficient when practicing the presence of God! And the cold? I could feel it ebbing away round about Birmingham. By the time I reached Bushey there was not a trace of it. Nor was there any trace of it during the course or after it. I find it very difficult to attribute this sequence of events to coincidence. For a clergyman I have a well-developed capacity for doubt and skepticism, but so often tangible results follow healing prayer. See for yourself. The ring of God's peace is waiting for you.

6/Why Did One Man Live and the Other Man Die?

Perhaps this is the right point to look at a problem which is inevitably raised by an honest consideration of Christian healing, a problem to which so far I have found no completely satisfactory solution—the problem of the unhealed. Put in a nutshell the difficulty is this: if Christian healing sometimes works in a physical sense, why does it not always do so?

I can highlight this problem by telling two contrasting stories. In a parish where I used to work, one of my church wardens had to go into the hospital for an operation. Something went wrong and instead of improving afterward he became steadily worse. He could not eat. His weight loss was appalling. One of the doctors told me he had no chance of recovery. But he was wrong. We organized widespread prayer for him. I prayed with him in the hospital and administered a laying on of hands. And against all the odds he started to eat again and to recover strength. His recovery was complete and he went on to serve as a vigorous church warden for a further ten years.

Contrast the story of a member of another parish—in many ways a closely similar story. He too underwent an operation. Afterward his condition became markedly worse. He could not eat. There was an appalling weight loss. I was told he had no chance of recovery. He was expected to die early in 1972. Again widespread prayer was organized. I prayed with him and administered a laying on of hands. He started to eat and to recover strength. The spring, summer and autumn of 1972 passed and then quite suddenly in November he died. It was true that he had lived six bonus months, that the end was peaceful and that both he and his wife received extraordinary strength of spirit. She is still a strong, positive influence in the life of the church. But the fact remains that he died.

Why did one man live and the other die? There was no lack of faith on the part of the second man and his wife. What then? I cannot believe those who suggest that sometimes God arbitrarily chooses to heal, sometimes not to heal. God never ceases to be "the Lord, your healer." He does not change.

If I had to attempt an answer to the enigma, it would be something like this. There are laws governing the universe; laws of logic, laws of nature, laws of life. We are beginning to have a better understanding of some of them but there is much to learn. God does not break these laws. They are part of his own nature. When we pray for physical healing and it does not happen, some factor within these laws is preventing it. There would be no need to heal in a perfect world, but this sinful world is far from perfect and contains many a block to healing. Very often we cannot see where the block lies. It may not be in the sufferer at all. For myself I am sure that it never lies in God.

This obviously does not constitute a complete or satisfactory answer, but the facts are that sometimes physical healing follows prayer and the laying on of hands, sometimes it does not. It does no honor to the Lord of truth to deny these facts or to produce explanations which are glib or superficial.

There are a few practical points which may be added. They do not answer the problem but they do help in actually coping with a situation of sickness. Perhaps also they help to indicate some of the blocks which can hinder healing.

1. *It is not helpful to long too much for purely physical healing. One can overpray at a physical level.* As a ministrant one can communicate more of one's own anxiety than of the calm strong love of Christ. As a patient one can actually resist the healing process by keeping one's attention on the need for it to take place. Insomnia provides a simple illustration. Longing to go to sleep, striving to go to sleep is no help at all. Praying to go to sleep may not be much better. But accept that sleeping or waking you can offer the night to God, relax in his presence, enjoy his acceptance, his peace, his love, his healing, know that you are in his arms and the odds are that once you stop looking for sleep, it comes looking for you.

2. *Physical health, while it is a lovely God-willed thing, is not the whole or the deepest part of health.* At our mission of teaching and healing a young wife, who I will call Melanie, came forward for a laying on of hands. She was a keen Christian but bitter because she was suffering from multiple sclerosis. Afterward the multiple sclerosis seemed untouched but the bitterness had gone. It would be wrong to say that there was no healing.

In fact, what happened to Melanie illustrates a further principle: complete healing often takes place over a long period of time. Some months after she received our ministry of Christian healing she became aware of small improvements in her condition. Within a year the hospital she attended as an outpatient noticed the improvement too. She was told she was "going into remission" and physiotherapy was prescribed to help her make the most of it. Gradually it became clear that this was much more than a remission. The improvement continued. Melanie got out of her wheelchair and back onto two crutches, and then found she could manage with one cane, and then that she did not need a cane at all. She was able to walk—and walk normally. She went hiking! She played tennis! After eleven years off work she started work again. The hospital stopped her treatment and told her she could no longer be said to have multiple sclerosis. All the side effects disappeared. Beforehand she suffered from double vision. This has now become normal. Beforehand her speech was slurred. Now it is crystal clear.

3. *Christian healing does not actually focus the mind on ailments but on positive spiritual truth.* One of my congregation expressed some disquiet when we started with services of healing. He was afraid they would turn us into hypochondriacs. I could see the point, but he had got it wrong. When we minister the laying on of hands in the name of Christ at a service, we do not put our minds on the troubles of the people who are kneeling at the communion rail, but we fill our minds with the picture of the risen Christ.

If you are ill it is good not to think too much about the ailments but to focus attention on a healing sequence of ideas and to go through them again and again. For instance, each person of the Holy Trinity can provide a healing train of thought.

God the Father made me—he loves me—the creative energies of God are around me and in me. Jesus healed the sick—he is alive today—he has not changed—he still heals —and he is with me now. Come, Holy Spirit—you are the giver of life and health—come into every part of me—let your healing power move in me, work in me, live in me— overflow from me, use me in the healing of the world.

In thought sequences such as these Christ will touch

us and though we may be ill he will do us good. The illness may not be better, but *we* shall be better. Maybe both. But it is better not to dictate the form of healing he will bring.

4. *We shall not know the full possibilities of healing by the power of Christ in the church of Christ, till the church as a whole takes Christian healing much more seriously.* I am sure that we and the world are suffering from lack of faith and lack of commitment on the part of the church as a whole. If your left leg wanted to step forward but your right leg did not, you would do the splits rather than make progress. The church is rather like that. It is a divided body, some members stepping forward, others dithering or falling back. We have the command of Christ: "heal." What are we waiting for?

5. *In the meantime remember that God can bring good out of any situation, even sickness and death.* He can bring good out of it whether physical healing comes or not. "We know that in everything God works for good with those who love him" (Rom. 8:28). It is important to look for the blessing, the positive opportunity, the golden thread in the worst situation—to look for it, thank God for it, and offer it trustingly in his service. It is surprising how much good can come out of bad times. The ultimate example must be Calvary. Nothing could have seemed worse. Physical pain, mental agony, spiritual dereliction—but God used it to redeem the world!

7/Why Does a God of Love Allow Suffering?

One of my early parishes was full of children. It was said that elderly people kept off the streets for fear of being run down by baby carriages! With so many children around sometimes one came across appalling tragedies. One of the worst occurred when a young father ran over his baby in his drive. He had several children and, when he was backing his car out of the garage, he usually kept a close watch on them to see that they were not in the way. But one day he failed to see that his youngest child, still a baby, had crawled behind the car. He knew about this only when his rear wheels went over the baby's body. The father was in a terrible state afterward, as was the mother. When I visited her, she lay in bed moaning over and over again, "What did I do to deserve it? What sin did I commit? Why has God punished me like this?"

It is a question that recurs in one form or another

throughout the life of a clergyman. I remember it being asked soon after I became a curate when I had to take the funeral of a young child who had died from cancer. I was asked it again a few days before I wrote this chapter.

A woman sat in my study. Her husband whom she adored had died of a heart attack soon after retiring. "Why did God take him?" she asked. "What wrong had he done? He was a good man. He deserved better than this." She was full of bitterness. She admitted she had been railing against God, blaspheming, cursing the God whom she believed was responsible. I tried to tell her, as I have tried to tell many others, that God is a God of life and health and joy, not of suffering, disease and tragic premature death. So where do these things come from?

There seem to be three types of suffering. First, there is the suffering which we bring upon ourselves. For instance, if I drink myself silly and the next morning have a hangover, I have only myself to blame. It is what the army calls "a self-inflicted wound." Much venereal disease must come into the same category.

Second, there is the suffering which we bring on each other. This is a most extensive category. It includes obvious instances like the drunken driver who knocks over a pedestrian and injures him. The injury is not the pedestrian's doing, but neither is it God's doing. It is a man-made situation caused by the interaction of one person with another. Again venereal disease is not only a "self-inflicted wound." One person infects another with it. Parents pass it to their children.

In thinking of types of suffering which we bring on each other, we must also include those diseases for which we have a collective responsibility as members of society and of the human race. Many stress diseases, many road accidents, and diseases connected with the misuse and pollution of the world in which we live are of this sort. They are experienced individually but caused collectively. So are malnutrition diseases which are completely unnecessary in a world as rich in resources as ours. So are all the horrors associated with war.

The third category simply consists of types of suffering which seem not to come under the first two headings. Actually, this is a rapidly diminishing category. With increasing knowledge we are continually able to move individual types of disease or suffering from the third group to the first or second. For instance, till recently no cause was known for lung cancer, but now we know that we can bring it on ourselves by smoking and bring it on each other by polluting the atmosphere.

It would seem that though we live in a universe where there is a certain amount of built-in risk, the greater part of disease and suffering is demonstrably manmade in one way or another. However, if God does not cause it himself, there is still a problem. Why does he allow man to cause it?

Strangely the answer seems to be connected with God's *love*. If God is love, then it is to be expected that he will create and that he will wish to love his creatures. Man was created to be loved by God, to explore and enjoy and reflect that love. But in order to love and be loved he had to be free. You can't love a robot or a puppet. So man was given free will. Free will is the most wonderful gift in the world. God actually restricted his own freedom when he gave it— a miracle in itself. But it is also the most terrible gift in the world. If it is a genuine gift, we must be free to use it or misuse it. We can love and serve God or we can play at being our own god and reject love and replace it with selfishness, greed and hate. We can hurt ourselves and hurt each other.

Free will is a dangerous thing, but if God were to take it away, he would destroy us. We would no longer be people. So God leaves us our free will and we use it stupidly, sinfully, to bring suffering into the world. Sometimes we cause suffering just through ignorance, by accident. Freedom is a hazardous business. But if the risks are great, the positive potentialities are beyond conception. There is a risk of self-destruction, but there is a potential for glory which defies description. This is particularly so when one sets the whole issue in the context of eternity as we shall seek to do later.

One further thing must be said in discussing the problem of suffering. If God allows suffering this does not mean that he acquiesces in it. Having given us free will God has not washed his hands of us. He is not just an interested bystander watching to see whether the human race will make the grade or whether we shall be our own unmaking. Without diminishing human free will, without manipulating us or coercing us in any way, God is a God of involvement, a God of healing. The creative energies of the Father are all around us and deep within us, rich in healing power. Jesus is a living redemptive healing reality, freely available to all who will open themselves to him. The Holy Spirit, Lord of life and health, is the greatest gift of all time. It is for us to accept or reject the healing power of God, to cooperate with him or to resist him. The problem of suffering is not only an issue to be discussed, it is more than an academic problem, it is a battlefield, a call to action, a challenge to involvement, an opportunity for healing.

So far this chapter has been necessarily speculative, but it seems right to end it in a practical way. What can we say to any who at this moment are undergoing a time of personal tragedy or suffering and who feel confused or bitter about it? Who ask, "Why should it happen to me?" Here are five thoughts which, I believe, have healing in them for people who feel this way.

1. It is useful to turn the question round and ask, "Why should it *not* happen to me?" If we live in a world where for one reason or another suffering is a fact of life, why should it *not* happen to me? Why should suffering always be reserved for the other fellow? Why should I be immune? What is so special about me? Certainly it would be nice to have an immunity badge, but Jesus never promised one to his followers. He promised not immunity but victory,

which is a different thing.

2. If it is in your heart to rage against God, then rage away. God can do something with honest rage. He can do nothing with pretended piety. I sometimes recommend to my startled congregation the practice of "swear prayers." When the world seems intolerable and you feel sick and angry, say so honestly and in your own language. God knows you feel like that anyway, so why not say so? I said this to the woman who was in my study a few days ago, raging at the loss of her husband. Even though God did not himself will the premature death of her husband, he will not back away from her rage. He will not answer rage with condemnation or rejection. So picture God in Christ hanging on the cross. Let your rage ram the crown of thorns on. Let your rage hammer in the nails. He will still love you.

3. Know that God understands, really understands. Part of the message of the cross of Jesus is that God understands suffering from the inside. He suffers when we suffer. When I celebrated Holy Communion in the side chapel at St. George's, Hyde, before me was a cross which was given in 1920 by some parents who had lost their seventeen-year-old son. In the loss of their son they turned to the God who had lost his own son, and in their minds they held the two events together. I hope they found healing in doing so.

4. Don't resist healing by overcherishing bitterness. It is easy to clutch a grudge against the universe, to refuse to let it go, but it does no good. Be ready for healing when it comes whether it comes through time, or through the love of family and friends, or specifically through the love and power of Jesus.

5. When you have finally found a way of facing the situation and you can cope with life again, watch out for others who are still enmeshed by personal suffering or tragedy. In a unique way you will be able to help them from the reserve of your own experience.

8/Medicine and Religion

In the previous two chapters we have looked at two large problems: Why does Christian healing sometimes bring a physical cure and sometimes not? And why do suffering and disease exist at all if God is loving and good?

We turn now to a further problem, that of the relationship between Christian healing and medical science. Fortunately, unlike the other two, this really is hardly a problem at all, or so I reckon. I fail to see why logically there should be any sort of clash between Christian healing and medical science. One of my happiest experiences of healing involved close step-by-step cooperation with a local doctor as together we tried to bring healing to a teen-age girl suffering from a particularly unpleasant skin condition. We can call her Betty.

Betty lived with her parents, worked in a bank and was a

regular communicant member of the Church of England. She was also a picture of misery.

One day after church I asked her if she would like to talk about whatever it was that troubled her and she arranged to come to see me. She told me she had not been at all well. She had been in the hospital with vulvitis (inflammation and irritation of the genital area) and the treatment there had not seemed to help in any way. Her mental condition was bad—she was forgetful, unable to concentrate, completely unhopeful, acutely unhappy, afraid of going mad.

Subsequently I spent an hour talking with her family doctor, and we both felt that there was an underlying anxiety condition which needed to be recognized and healed. We agreed that I should try to help her. In all, I saw her eight times for about an hour and a half on each occasion. There was a break in the middle of these interviews while she saw a psychiatrist, but the psychiatrist suggested that she should come back to me. Month by month we talked about her life: her childhood, her relationship with her parents, her fears, her loneliness. We found she was very much afraid of sex—afraid of marriage, of intercourse, of childbirth. My wife joined in some of the discussions, and gradually as Betty came to trust us, she admitted to us and to herself the roots of her fears, which lay in some rather unpleasant childhood experiences.

We spoke a great deal about the nature of Christian security, founded on the love of God and his acceptance of us and identification with us. Each interview ended with prayer, a blessing and the laying on of hands. At every point the family doctor knew what was happening.

Gradually both the vulvitis and the underlying anxiety lessened their grip. There was an interim period during which Betty would be free from the vulvitis for a day or two and then it would return. It would come and go, and we could actually recognize the various anxiety stimulants which produced it and the positive thought patterns which soothed it away. Finally it cleared. Now many years later

Betty is a happy, well-adjusted wife and mother. It was a seal upon her healing when one day she said, "If ever it would help anybody else for you to tell them about me, I shan't mind."

It was good to be in contact with the medical profession throughout all this. Betty's condition was such a delicate one that I would not have been happy unless I had medical contacts. I still have letters from Betty's family doctor and from the psychiatrist to whom he sent her. They both approved the treatment which I was giving. In addition I spoke to the gynecologist who treated her in the hospital and to another psychiatrist for a second opinion. It was all very much a team effort. When Betty's self-revelations looked as though they might be somewhat traumatic the psychiatrist prescribed suitable tablets. When Betty's parents, who were not altogether in sympathy with the church at that time, expressed disquiet the family doctor visited them and allayed their fears. My wife was able to play her part all the more effectively because she is a trained physiotherapist who has specialized in antenatal care. We all worked together.

Medical and spiritual treatment often go hand in hand. A clerical colleague recently told me that on a visit to a local hospital he was asked to pray with a patient who was semiconscious and very restive and troubled. He prayed briefly and administered a laying on of hands. The patient at once went to sleep. He had been under drugs for four days, but only at that point did they become properly operative. The medical needed the spiritual to complete it.

Perhaps I may add a further rather personal example. A month before I wrote this chapter my wife's father died. He went into the hospital for an operation, apparently survived the operation well, but died three days later, suddenly, from a heart attack. When my wife and I reached her mother, we found that not only was she very shaken by events at the hospital but also she was steadily becoming covered from head to foot in ugly painful lumps and blotches. The doctor said it was an allergy of some kind. He prescribed tablets. They had no effect. He added a prescription for ointment. It made no difference. He changed the treatment from tablets to capsules. The condition became worse than ever and it was decided to try the tablets again.

At this point I had a strong urge to pray with my mother-in-law and to administer a laying on of hands in the name of Christ. It was late at night, but I went to her bedroom and asked if she would allow me to do so. She said she had been trying to pluck up courage to ask me to do so all day, so we spent five or ten minutes in prayer and then I put my hands on her head and commended her to the healing power of our Lord. Next morning the condition had started to improve.

By the time that the funeral took place thirty-six hours later, the condition was so much better that none of the mourners would have noticed anything had been wrong with her. The tablets, it seemed, were at last doing her good, but there was no sign whatsoever that they were doing so until she received a laying on of hands in the name of Christ. Again the spiritual complemented and completed the medical.

Betty's family doctor told me that early in his practice he had learned the importance of an element in healing which was not strictly medical. He was called to the bedside of a sick old lady whom he knew well and who trusted and respected him completely. As he entered the room she said, "I shall feel better now, doctor," and as he sat by her bedside holding her hand her racing pulse slowed down under his fingers until it became absolutely normal. He realized at that point that there was no medical reason for the improvement in the condition which was taking place before his eyes and under his hands. He said to me that he knew in that moment that there was more to healing than pills and a stethoscope.

If the presence and the touch of a trusted family doctor

can do so much, how much more can the presence and touch of Christ. Healing by touch is an old and honored form of therapy. Every mother knows it by instinct. Many a doctor learns it from experience. It is sad that the church has forgotten or disregarded it to such an extent for so long in spite of the evidence around us and in spite of the specific injunction of Christ.

Sometimes, of course, when a local church arouses itself to take an interest in Christian healing after years of comparative inactivity in this sphere, local doctors may regard the development with suspicion. There may be various reasons for this. One is that they just are not used to it. Another, that they may have come across fringe sects doing strange things—Jehovah's Witnesses refusing to allow their children to receive blood transfusions or Christian Scientists refusing drugs or other remedies or spiritualists practicing so-called psychic surgery. Doctors may not realize that these bodies are as unorthodox *theologically* as they are *medically*. And of course a third reason is that doctors, like the rest of us, are not free from prejudice. Christian healing may arouse it.

If we come across suspicion on the part of doctors, we should be patient, be ready to explain the point and practice of Christian healing not just in terms of Scripture but in terms of reason and experience, be ready to deal with objections carefully and in detail. When the moment comes that we are offered the opportunity to cooperate in healing we must take it with both hands.

In Hyde some of the doctors at the health center were suspicious when we started our services of "Investigation into Christian Healing." One church member who went to see her doctor was told, "Why come here? Why not go to that healing service of yours?" and at the Mission of Teaching and Healing, although the physiotherapists from the local clinic were well represented not a single doctor from the health center attended any of the meetings so far as we could see. However, gradually doctors are coming to see that we are not claiming any magical powers. There is no mumbo jumbo. Nobody is being harmed and many are being helped. It was a great day when a doctor first told one of his patients, "I think you should go to the St. George's service of healing." As it was when a doctor phoned me and said, "I think that perhaps you can help such and such a patient better than I can. May I arrange an appointment for her to see you?" I was delighted when two doctors came to the vicarage for an evening to discuss the whole concept of Christian healing, and even more delighted when the same two doctors subsequently attended one of our "Rediscovery of Christian Healing" services. As they left, one of them commented to an usher, "I hope I shall be a better doctor for being here tonight." Before I started to write this chapter, one of my congregation phoned me to tell me of a splendid piece of concern and healing on the part of that doctor. I hope I shall be a better pastor for having heard of that! We can help and encourage each other so much, we who have the privilege of serving the healing professions. That is the way it should be.

9/The Healing of Relationships

It cannot be said too often that Christian healing is not just concerned with the body but with the person as a totality, life as a whole. It follows that it must be concerned with the healing of relationships.

I remember once spending the early hours of the morning with a couple who had attended one of our Christian healing services and had received the laying on of hands. They had a fair enough marriage, but like many married couples they irritated each other in various ways. Each bottled up a sense of irritation at the other, but each was blissfully unaware of the irritation caused to the other. After the service the wife felt moved to uncork the bottle and tell her husband of the ways in which he irritated her. He returned the compliment. The exchange became more and more heated. In the end he became so angry that he smashed a vase which had been given them as a wedding present. She went to bed sobbing and threatening divorce. The husband sat for half an hour gazing at the fragments of the vase and wondering how in the world all this could have followed a service of healing! Then he telephoned me and asked me to come over.

We sat around the bed, he in his shirt sleeves, she in her nightgown. He told me what she had said about him. She told me what he had said about her.

"Are they true, these things you have heard about yourselves?" I asked. And here the grace of God showed itself.

Quite simply they both said, "Yes."

"And have you loved each other over the years?" I asked.

"We don't talk about that sort of thing," they said.

"Have you loved each other?" I persisted.

"Yes," they admitted.

"Tell each other so," I commanded, highly autocratic.

"I've loved her. I still do," said the husband.

"Don't tell me, tell your wife," I said.

Hesitantly, gropingly he started to speak to her of his love, and she did the same. Putting my best quasi-medical manner on, I prescribed that they should say, "I love you" at least once a week for the rest of their lives and I threatened to check up on it.

They have almost had a second honeymoon since then. There are two new elements in their marriage: articulated love and absolute honesty. Before I left, we all prayed, and it was remarkable to hear them acknowledging and thanking God for the healing and deepening of their relationship. The marriage is now one of the strongest I know.

There was a similar healing in the life of Tess who received the laying on of hands at one of our services. It felt, she told me later, as though the hands on her head were red-hot, burning her like coals. Next month she came again. Two different people were administering the laying on of hands, but again the hands were red-hot. She prayed

about it and came to the conclusion that there was something in her life which God wanted to purge, to burn away.
It was her normal custom to justify herself. "They're all out
of step but our Tess," was her motto. But now honestly and
thoroughly she examined herself—and she admitted the
result to me and to her husband. "I'm so ashamed," she
said, but almost under our eyes healing was taking place.
She is more of a whole person now and her marriage is the
better for it.

Of course we ought not to rely on "red-hot" hands to
produce this result in every case. There are many ways in
which the church can be a channel of healing. Premarriage
preparation, honest life-centered preaching and the family
life of the church as a whole should be geared to be helpful and healing in the sphere of marriage relationships.

Another area of relationships in which there is often
need for healing is the attitude which we have to our parents, even to parents now dead. A wrong attitude to parents can underlie many a mentally or physically sick condition. Judy was a young wife who seemed incapable of
getting up before eleven in the morning and never started
her housework till four in the afternoon. Underneath this
practice was a stressed and sick attitude to her mother,
now dead.

"I loathed my mother," she said. "She was domineer-
ing, house-proud without having anything to be proud
about, a magistrate, always giving orders, always so superior. She took all the guts out of me."

Whether this was a true picture, that was how Judy saw
it. And there was no healing for her till she had forgiven
her mother. There was Agnes who had a marriage problem. Behind it was the memory of her father who used to
walk around the house naked and had a sexual attitude toward her and asked her to masturbate him after she was
about eight years old.

To a young child, mother and father are like gods, the
source of life, love, sustenance, standards and security. But

people are not perfect. Parents are flawed gods. We all have much to thank our parents for, but we all have something to forgive them for also. Thanking and forgiving in correct proportions, demoting parents from gods to human beings like ourselves, this is part of growing into maturity. Spiritual healing is sometimes needed before we can achieve it.

Christ wants to touch our relationship with our neighbors too. But, like other forms of Christian healing, he never forces it upon us. Perhaps I may include a cautionary tale here. In a parish where I used to work there were two women who could not stand each other. One had a dog which had bitten the other one's son. She justified it by saying that her dog was a very good judge of character! The relationship had gone from bad to worse.

I brought them into church, asked them to kneel down, and suggested that they each forgive each other and ask each other's forgiveness. But it was *my* bright idea not theirs. They did not want it at all. Within ten minutes after one had called on me, the other telephoned to say, "That woman didn't mean a word of it." There was no healing at all. You cannot preach the gospel at the point of a gun. You cannot bring healing to those who are determined not to be healed.

I suppose this is why the healing power of Christ is not more evident in interclass and intergroup relationships within society. Christ has his hand stretched out to heal, but we have not yet come to the point where we want his healing. We hold on to our own greed and sectional interests. We can see that something is wrong but we have not yet come to the point of repentance, the point of making ourselves available and accessible to Christ's healing power.

There are, however, signs that this may be beginning to happen within the church itself. I have already written about the new unity which our mission of teaching and healing brought to some of the churches in Hyde. At one meeting following the mission a key member of a local

Protestant church stood up and said he now realized he had been sick for years. The name of the sickness was prejudice. For years he had supposed that the gospel was the sole property of his own church. He had thought of the Church of England as hostile to or at any rate irrelevant to the gospel. He wanted to tell us how wrong he had been and how much joy he now felt in the new friendship we were sharing.

I particularly remember sitting in a car with the vicar of a neighboring church. Each of us was moved to admit how much had been wrong with the relationship between our churches and ourselves. From that time on the relationship has been healed.

So often the division between one church and another, the disunity among denominations, is not primarily theological but sociological and downright sin centered, based on pride, prejudice and preconditioning. The power of Christian healing can work wonders here. If we allow forces of healing to grow in the church, we shall see a new unity, a new strength and a new capacity for bringing the healing of relationships to our sick society.

10/The Healing of Anxiety

When Bishop Taylor Smith was asked to write something in an autograph book, he often used to write this:

The worried cow would have lived till now
If she had saved her breath,
But she feared her hay wouldn't last all day
And she mooed herself to death!

I am told that the word "worry" comes from an Anglo-Saxon word meaning "wolf." Certainly worry can be like a wolf in the way it tears at life. Not that it tears the troubles from tomorrow. What it does is to tear the strength and peace from today.

Anxiety is useless, dangerous and very common. Our age has been called "the age of anxiety." So if the Christian church has a gospel for today, a gospel which heals, it must be seen to speak relevantly and effectively to the many folk who are fettered by anxiety.

There are two types of anxiety. First, there is anxiety about a specific object. Bishop Taylor Smith's worried cow knew what she was worrying about and so do many anxious men and women. "Will I get the job I want?" "Will I pass my exam?" "Will I be all right when I go into the hospital?" "Are my children all right, now that they are living away from home?" and so on.

Second, there is another sort of anxiety, a deeper sort, which does not seem to have a specific object at all. Milly comes into my mind. She is a natural worrier. She has to have something to worry about. If there is no handy problem around, she will invent something, because the worry is deep inside her.

Or I think of Poppy who because she is deep-down anxious cannot bear to be ignored. She has to be the center of attention. At first glance she looks self-confident, but those who know her well can see that behind the attention seeking there is deep anxiety which cannot face being really alone.

Then there is Alexander who is afraid of deep friendships, afraid of being hurt and so always keeps his distance. He looks self-sufficient, but underneath it all he is not secure enough to trust another person. One day his self-sufficiency may crack, and if that happens he will be in for a nervous breakdown.

Deep insecurity is common, commoner than one might think, because we do not like to admit it and so we try to hide it, even from ourselves. But of course hiding something does not make it go away. The anxiety lurks under the surface and affects our behavior in strange and painful ways.

How specifically can the healing power of Christ be brought to bear on an anxiety condition? Anxiety about a specific object, though it can be agonizing, is the easier sort to deal with. The rule of thumb which my wife and I worked out when our younger son was ill as a baby was

Do your best
And leave the rest
to God

This means taking the best practical action humanly possible, but at the same time putting the whole situation, including the ultimate outcome, in the hands of God. On a number of occasions people who have received a laying on of hands at one of our services have reported afterward, "I had this or that problem before the service, but now I have decided not to worry about it anymore. I'll do what I can and then leave it with God."

It reminds me of King Hezekiah taking the sneering menacing letter which he had received from Sennacherib the Assyrian (2 Kings 19) and spreading it out in the house of the Lord before God. In effect he prayed, "Lord, you are very great and very strong. Take this situation into your hands. I'll do what I can but I will leave the issue with you." It was a powerful prayer then. It is a powerful prayer now.

But what when we do not have a letter to spread before God? What when there is no external problem which we can commit to him—but just an inner emptiness? This sort of faceless anxiety can dominate and ruin life. How does the Christian faith offer healing here?

I believe there is a basic threefold truth which we need to appropriate for ourselves. God made me. God loves me. God wants me. He made me and no creation of his is valueless. He loves me even to the point of the cross. He wants me and he has something for me to do and to be in his service.

There is a deep healing power in this threefold truth. I watched it, for instance, healing Betty, the girl whose skin condition concealed an underlying anxiety state. I watched it healing Edwina, a nervous middle-aged woman who could hardly look life or her husband in the face because of her feelings of anxiety and worthlessness. Her husband thought much more of her when she began to think more of herself. And speaking personally one of the joys of my life has been that of seeing my own deep anxiety lift from my shoulders as the threefold truth has become more and more a part of me.

The healing is a gradual process. Anxiety tends to be a deeply ingrained element in our personality with roots going back to the earliest months of life, perhaps even to the birth process itself. There is good news here and bad news. The good news is that Jesus has revealed a God who made, loves and wants us. There is healing and hope. The bad news is that the healing can be expected to take time, it may even take a lifetime. That is almost the whole story —almost, but not quite. There is a postscript which can come as a personal miracle to the anxiety sufferer.

It is usual to think of anxiety as an enemy, and so it is. But when the enemy is offered to God, it has a strange way of turning into a friend. As St. Paul says in Romans 8:28, "... in everything God works for good with those who love him"—even in anxiety.

There are at least three ways in which God uses anxiety for our good, while he is gently and steadily healing it, loving it away. First, anxiety when it is recognized and accepted and offered to God can be a bulwark against the worst of all sins, the sin of pride, the folly of supposing that I can lead an adequate life centered on myself. Every twinge of anxiety can be a signal to me that man finds rest only in God.

Second, anxiety can help me to understand others, to stand where they stand. For there are precious few people totally unscarred by it.

Third, those who know they are anxious can, I believe, experience the companionship of Christ in a unique way. On the cross Christ cried those mysterious words, "My God, my God, why hast thou forsaken me?" (Mk. 15:34). God was his whole being; Christ knew what it was to lose his being in dread and dereliction. If we have to enter into deep pains of anxiety, however deeply we may go, Christ will always have penetrated more deeply. He offers himself as our companion on the way, our guide, our fellow sufferer. The companionship of Christ is, to my knowledge, the most precious gift in the world. It may well be that within eternity those who have known the deepest anxiety in Christ's companionship will be regarded as the most fortunate of all.

Perhaps this gives some clue to the meaning of the first beatitude. "Blessed are the poor in spirit [literally, "those whose spirits are full of cringing fear"!] for [incredibly!] *theirs* is the *kingdom of heaven*" (Mt. 5:3).

11/Case History of an Angry Man

I shall never forget Greg. He used to sit near the back of the church. He turned up week after week, never really looking happy, sometimes looking positively depressed. He stopped coming for a while but started again—still looking depressed. One day as I looked through my window I saw him pacing up and down on the road outside. He did this for several minutes and rather belatedly it struck me that he was plucking up courage to come and talk to me. I went to the front door and simultaneously he must have found his courage because we met there.

"I don't know why I've come," he said. "You can't help me. Nobody can."

I invited him in and he came into my study where he sat for minutes without saying anything, his head in his hands.

In the end he spoke. "I feel so rotten and ill," he said. He told me he had feelings of tension in his head, he could not breathe properly because his nose was continually congested, he had a tight feeling across his chest, his heart pounded away, he sweated all the time (he was certainly sweating at the moment), he could not sleep at night, he could not concentrate by day, his fingernails were bitten down, he looked as though the world was on his shoulders.

Gradually he started to talk about his life. By any standards he had not had the easiest of lives. When he was thirteen years old, his mother died. When he was eighteen, his father died. When he was nineteen, he married a lovely girl, the apple of his eye. She died of cancer when he was twenty-three. He had married again but now his second wife, like his first, had become ill, and seemed not to be making progress.

He had had a series of unsatisfactory jobs. In one of them there was an accounting error and he came under suspicion. Although he was completely cleared he felt he had to leave. In his present job he did not get on with the head of his department. Because of feeling ill, his standard of work had slipped and his superior had reprimanded him. He was afraid he might be sacked. He had gone to his doctor, but his doctor told him there was nothing wrong with him and he must pull himself together.

He had always gone to church and believed in the God of the Ten Commandments, a God of judgment. He did not enjoy church, but on the one occasion on which he missed, he was involved in a road accident and ended up in a ditch, which he took as a warning from God. He could see no way out of his ill health, his problems at home, his problems at work—except perhaps one.

On a hunch I asked him if he had ever thought of putting an end to it all. He covered his face again and admitted that he thought of suicide more and more.

By this time we had spent nearly two hours together and

I felt the need to think and pray. I asked him to come again at a set time the next day and made him promise that until then at any rate he would put aside thoughts of suicide. I also told him that he had been right to come to me and that a solution to his troubles might be nearer than he thought.

Next day it seemed right to feed the situation back to him and to interpret it to some extent. On the surface he looked depressed and burdened. But underneath it he must, I felt, be suppressing a great deal of anger. This is often so in cases of depression and I wanted to see if I could bring it into the open.

"I'm not surprised," I said, "that you are feeling fed up with life. If I were you I'd be smoldering about it. Just think... ," and I led him back through the death of his mother, his father and his first wife, his wife's illness, the unfair treatment in his former job, the unfair treatment in his present job.

"Do you know," I said innocently, "if you bottle up this sort of anger it can make you feel ill in all sorts of ways?" I took down a textbook from a shelf and started reading a list of the sort of symptoms which suppressed anger can produce: head tension, nasal congestion, tightness of the chest, heart pounding, sweating, insomnia. They were all his symptoms.

At this point, for the first time he let his anger out and he directed it initially against his doctor. He stood up and strode about the room. For a time I thought he was going to break something. He was so furious. "That bloody doctor," he shouted, "he should have known, he should have told me."

I let him rage away for a time and then said, "Perhaps you are right to be cross about your doctor, but face it, you're not just angry with your doctor, you're angry with life itself." He admitted it. "And that means," I said, "that you're angry with *God*."

Suddenly he was quiet. He did not like this as an idea because his idea of God was of a hard, judging god, a god of rules, regulations and requirements, a god who knocks you into a ditch if you stop going to church for a while. However, I was able to show him that that sort of god was a god in his own head, not the God revealed to us by Jesus. I took him to the cross and we saw together that even when we ram down the crown of thorns and knock in the nails Christ goes on loving and that this is what God is like. I encouraged him to take his anger and his total experience of life to the cross and leave them there. We prayed and I administered a laying on of hands.

Soon after, Greg attended an evangelistic service and on the basis of his new-found understanding of himself and of God, he went forward as an act of commitment to the true God whom he was beginning to know and trust.

I saw him for a final appointment about a fortnight later. He was a changed man. His depression had gone. His health troubles had gone. His concentration was back. His supervisor at work was so surprised by the change in his work that he checked to see whether his colleagues were doing it for him! "I wouldn't have thought it possible that I could be so changed," he said. We thanked God for it together. Two years later he left the parish, but before going he came to see me and said very simply, "Before I go I want to tell you that you have saved my life."

I have told this story in detail because it takes us to the heart of Christian healing. Underlying Greg's bodily symptoms, his feelings of depression, his difficulties in dealing with the people around him and in coping with life as a whole, was the fact that he was not right with God. His relationship with God needed healing. This was also true of Betty, Tess, Judy, Agnes, Milly, Poppy, Alexander and in one sense or another of us all.

The heart of Christian healing lies not in the treatment of bodily ailments no matter how painful or tragic they may be. Basically it does not even lie in correcting man's attitude to his fellow man or man's attitude to himself, though in a fallen world both are wrong and sick. The deepest purpose of Christian healing is to right the relationship between man and God. Our wrong relationship with God is the ill which underlies all others. The heart of Christian wholeness lies in right-relatedness to God.

The healing work of Christ and the healing work of Christ's church is to minister wholeness and harmony with God to a divided and discordant world. The place from which this healing flows is supremely the cross of Christ—the cross on which he died and from which he rose triumphant. "And with his stripes we are healed" (Is. 53: 5). Greg found this true in his own experience. We can all find it true.

From the cross Christ offers us the saving relationship within which he bears the consequences of our sins and our rages, shares the depths of our anxieties and our fears, and tends the hurts of our bodies, minds and spirits. Each healing experience of the cross is unique, created by God with precision to bring forgiveness for our own individual sins, to meet perfectly our own individual needs and to restore in us that aspect of the image of God which is our true self.

12/Jesus Preaches... and Heals

The object of the sermon at our "Rediscovery of Christian Healing" service is always quite simply that of seeing and hearing Jesus. There can be no Christian healing without genuine contact with Christ.

The text which comes to mind again and again is, "Sir, we would see Jesus" (Jn. 12:21 KJV). It virtually comes before my eyes as I preach. There has to be real contact and it has to be with the real Christ. There are many common false notions about Christ and false pictures of him. If the word at these services is truly to be his word and the touch truly his touch these false ideas about Jesus must be dispelled.

For instance, there is the picture of Christ as a pale, unreal, stained-glass-window type of figure, whom you could never imagine sweating or laughing or living anything which could be recognized as ordinary life. There is no incarnation here and little healing. It is the product of bogus pietism. Or there is the idea, perhaps founded on a wrong interpretation of "Gentle Jesus, meek and mild," of a "sissy" Christ, who wouldn't say boo to a goose. Jesus could be gentle, of course, but he could also take a scourge and drive out of the temple those who were commercializing and exploiting religion.

There is the middle-class, respectable Christ, who comforts and buttresses conventional prejudice. That sort of Jesus does not accord with the evidence of Scripture. The real Jesus made it plain that he did not come to call the "respectable" (Lk. 5:32) and the leading citizens made it plain that they wanted to be rid of him (Lk. 19:47).

Or by contrast there is the left-wing, Che Guevara, guerrilla-type Christ, a political revolutionary, who would have had no sympathy with the respect which the real Jesus showed for civic and religious authority, and would not have wasted his time loving his enemies.

There is the narrow-minded, bigoted Christ who would never have gone to parties and who would have been keener to turn wine into water than vice versa. It is a startling thought that when the enemies of Jesus wanted to throw insults at him they called him a "glutton and a drunkard" (Mt. 11:19).

And there is the popular picture of Jesus as a good and kind homespun philosopher—whom nobody could possibly have wanted to crucify!—a sentimental rather than a scriptural Christ.

So what type of man was Jesus? The answer is that he defies typecasting. He was himself. The only way to answer the question, "What was Jesus like?" is to look at the evidence and let him speak for himself.

This is why at our Christian healing service we hand out copies of St. Luke's Gospel and work through it chapter by chapter, verse by verse, the hard parts as well as the easy parts, the uncongenial parts as well as those we happen to like. The object is to see Jesus as he was and as he is. This sort of preaching is not only full of surprises and full of healing for a congregation, it is also highly salutary for the preacher because most preachers tend to be selective in approaching Scripture and it is good to accept a framework which specifically excludes pre-selection and the distortion which can come with it.

This is a good point to stop talking about looking at Jesus and start actually doing it for a while. So here is a random passage from St. Luke's Gospel (5:12-32) and some of the thoughts which it brought to us when we considered it at a service.

Jesus has just called the first disciples and they have heard the call, left everything and followed him. Characteristically their first experience as followers is to see and marvel at Jesus as a healer.

"While he was in one of the cities, there came a man full of leprosy"—not necessarily someone whom modern doctors would describe as a leper, because the ancient world called various skin conditions leprosy. But the condition, whatever it was, was a serious and clearly visible one. He was full of it, says St. Luke, using the terminology which a doctor of those times would naturally employ. Poor man: physically he was a mess, socially he would be an outcast. All lepers were made to feel unwanted and unclean. Indeed the insecurity and lack of love could well have been an element in the condition.

"When he saw Jesus, he fell on his face and besought him, 'Lord, if you will you can make me clean.' And he stretched out his hand, and touched him, saying, 'I will; be clean.' "

The man did not doubt the power of Christ to heal, but he doubted the will of Christ to heal. This may seem strange but it still sometimes happens. It was how the housewife with the phobic condition in chapter three felt. She accepted without question that Christ could heal her.

The object of the counseling session was to make the point that she was precious to him, and that he not only could heal her but longed to do so. Once she had accepted this, the healing process had begun.

The touch of Christ upon the leper was a symbol of acceptance and security, powerful in the case of any ailment, but particularly powerful in conditions which render the sufferer socially unacceptable.

"Immediately the leprosy left him." The immediacy may surprise us, but skin conditions can react very quickly. We have seen how Betty, the girl with the vulvitis, found that at one stage of her experience of healing, her skin condition changed from day to day. Even more startling was the case of Janette, a young woman with an ugly skin condition which affected her hands, a condition which actually changed before my eyes as I was counseling her.

"And he charged him to tell no one; but 'go and show yourself to the priest, and make an offering for your cleansing, as Moses commanded, for a proof to the people.' " Normally Jesus tried to avoid publicity for his healings, and following this practice we have never advertised a service of healing, except in connection with the Mission of Teaching and Healing. Note the respect of Jesus for the old traditional ways of Leviticus 13 and 14, even though he himself was introducing new dimensions of life and healing to his followers.

In spite of his injunction to the leper, "so much the more the report went abroad concerning him; and great multitudes gathered to hear and to be healed of their infirmities. But he withdrew to the wilderness and prayed." And if he felt the need of prayer, how much more should we feel it in a ministry of healing. An important element in our local service consists of silent prayer undertaken by a group of worshipers beforehand in church. As others enter the building, they enter an atmosphere of prayer.

"On one of those days, as he was teaching, there were Pharisees and teachers of the law sitting by, who had come from every village of Galilee and Judea and from Jerusalem; and the power of the Lord was with him to heal." It seems that this was not always necessarily so. Jesus could experience blocks to healing just as we do.

"And behold, men were bringing on a bed a man who was paralyzed, and they sought to bring him in and lay him before Jesus; but finding no way to bring him in, because of the crowd...." In the story of the leper, the man had faith himself, but in the case of the paralytic it is friends who have faith. The crowd following Jesus was an actual hindrance here. I wonder how often those of us who reckon to follow Jesus are in fact an obstacle, blocking the way of others rather than helping them along the way.

The friends of the paralytic man were not put off by difficulties. "They went up on the roof and let him down with his bed through the tiles into the midst before Jesus." This really was friendship. Faith, friendship, foresight, flexibility and fortitude—we can find them all in the attitude of these men. At our services we find people with a similar persevering faith, working and praying for the healing of others.

"And when he saw their faith [the faith of the friends] he said, 'Man, your sins are forgiven.'" Paralysis can be caused by guilt. Where this is so, it can be dangerous to heal the paralysis without treating the guilt. Jesus recognized that this was the case here.

Note the underlying claim to authority in the words of Jesus. The scribes and Pharisees were certainly quick to see it. They seemed to have little concern for the paralyzed man himself but they pounced on the theological issue. They "began to question, saying, 'Who is this that speaks blasphemies? Who can forgive sins but God only?'" They saw the problem and were close to the solution, but they rejected it.

"Jesus perceived their questionings"—just as he perceived the guilt of the paralyzed man and the faith of the friends, and just as he knows your depths and mine.

" 'Which is easier, to say, "Your sins are forgiven you," or to say, "Rise and walk"?' " There was no answer. The process of heart hardening which was to be so obvious later in his ministry was beginning already.

To demonstrate that he did in fact have the authority to forgive sins Jesus commanded the paralytic man, "Take up your bed and go home." I would not dare to do this. My perception is not sharp enough. The flow of healing which comes through me is not sufficiently concentrated.

But Jesus knew what he was doing. "And immediately he rose before them, and took up that on which he lay, and went home, glorifying God. Amazement seized them all, and they glorified God and were filled with awe, saying, 'We have seen strange things today.' " The man praised God. The crowd praised God. The praise was as much a part of the miracle as the cure. Praising God and wholeness before God go together.

There is one further story of healing in the passage we are considering. At first sight it may not seem to be about healing, but Christian healing is not concerned exclusively, nor even primarily, with the body. "After this he went out and saw a tax collector, named Levi, sitting at the tax office." Tax collectors worked for the Roman occupying forces. They made a fat living by keeping part of the takings for themselves. They were known as cheats and traitors and were hated. Jesus said, "Follow me." Surprisingly, Levi "left everything, and rose and followed him." Jesus was in the process of turning one who had probably been a greedy, shady materialist into a man of God. Perhaps the most spectacular healing so far!

See what followed. "And Levi made him a great feast in his house; and there was a large company of tax collectors and others sitting at table with them." Levi had a ball. Accepting Christ's spiritual healing brings tremendous happiness. But the scribes and Pharisees were not happy. They muttered to the disciples and said, "Why do you eat and drink with tax collectors and sinners?" Again the heart-hardening process was in evidence and, unlike Levi, the scribes and Pharisees were not happy. There is no joy in resisting Christian insight and healing.

Jesus took their muttered question seriously and answered them. "Those who are well have no need of a physician, but those who are sick; I have not come to call the righteous, but sinners to repentance," not those who think themselves already good enough. The church is not a club for people with delusions of superiority. It is a hospital for sinners. Its business is healing at every level, just as this was the business of Jesus.

This has been no more than a glimpse of Jesus, twenty-one verses from one of the Gospels. It is about as much as can be fitted into a single service. But even a single glimpse of Jesus has healing in it and month-by-month glimpses of Jesus can build up into a good look at him. You may have heard the story of the old man who used to tell people that he reckoned he had been saved by having good looks. When anyone queried the statement, he expanded it by saying the good looks which save are good looks at Jesus —"Looking to Jesus the pioneer and perfecter of our faith" (Heb. 12:2).

Good looks at the good Lord—this is the essence of the receipt of life and health from Christ. It must be the essence of the message at any service of Christian healing.

13/Another Look
at Jesus

Let us continue to spend some time with "our eyes fixed on Jesus, on whom faith depends from start to finish," (Heb. 12:2 NEB), looking and listening to our healing Lord, with the help of Luke. We take up his story at the point at which we left it (5:33) and will stay with it till 6:19.

After his conversion Levi had a big party. He had met Jesus. He was happy. He wanted his friends and neighbors to meet Jesus and be happy too. But this seemed all wrong to some people. They said, "The disciples of John fast often and offer prayers, and so do the disciples of the Pharisees, but yours eat and drink." They thought that religious people should look severe, somber and strait-laced at all times. They remind me of a girl in my Sunday-school class who implored me just before my ordination, "Don't do it, Mr. Lawrence. Just think, you

won't never be able to have any fun anymore." A fine
Sunday-school teacher I had been! I had certainly failed
to communicate the joy and positiveness of the gospel to
her.

Of course there are occasions when Christians are called
to be sad. Because we are sinners we must be sorry for our
sins so that we may be receptive to our Father's forgiveness. Also, if we have any love in us, we shall sometimes
find ourselves called to share the world's suffering and
sadness in some way. And occasionally we may find ourselves in the doldrums because we are resisting God's will
in some way and the inner tussle produces a sort of thera-
peutic misery-patch until we have the sense to see that
God's way is best. But having said all that, it still remains
true that at the heart of Christian life and experience there
is joy—the joy of knowing Jesus, and through him the joy
of knowing that his Father is our Father, and his universe
is our home. All material things are fashioned by our
Father's hand—the food we eat and the beauties of nature
we enjoy. Our enjoyment of the world is part of our union
with Christ.

As Jesus put it, "Can you make wedding guests fast
while the bridegroom is with them?" Of course not,
though he added a dark hint of his coming crucifixion:
"The days will come, when the bridegroom is taken away
from them, and then they will fast in those days."

Then Jesus turned the conversation to a more important
matter than fasting, using, as so often, the parable method
to make his point. He said, "No one tears a piece from a
new garment and puts it upon an old garment; if he does,
he will tear the new, and the piece from the new will not
match the old. And no one puts new wine into old wine-
skins; if he does, the new wine will burst the skins and it
will be spilled, and the skins will be destroyed."

The point is that Christianity is not just the old Jewish
religion with one or two new ideas added. It is something
completely new. When a man becomes a committed Chris-

tian, he does not just add one or two new practices on to his old way of life. He becomes a new being. Christianity is a new coat, not an old coat with a new patch. It is new wine in a new bottle.

The gospel is concerned with conversion and new birth. "Therefore, if any one is in Christ, he is a new creation; the old has passed away, behold, the new has come" (2 Cor. 5:17). It is important that we should not tone down this concept. We are called to surrender old prejudices, old passions, old fears, old conceits, old negativities of body, mind and spirit. We are called to say, "Come Lord Jesus, come Holy Spirit, begin the work of new creation in me."

This work of new creation is the essence of Christian healing. We ought to be able actually to feel it in body, mind and spirit. If as you and I look back over the last twelve months we can see no evidence of new creation, new growth, new Christian dimensions in ourselves, then we should ask ourselves seriously whether something is wrong with our understanding of the faith or with the reality of our commitment to Christ.

The last verse of Luke 5 is a difficult one. It seems to contradict all that has gone before. "No one after drinking old wine desires new; for he says, 'The old is good.' " Mark and Matthew leave the verse out. So do some manuscripts of Luke's Gospel. But the words could well go back to Jesus. He went about doing the work of new creation, but he well understood those who would not receive that which he had to give. The verse forms a bridge between chapters 5 and 6, where we meet Pharisees who were so preoccupied with the law of Moses that they would not receive the gospel of Christ.

"On a sabbath, while he was going through the grain-fields, his disciples plucked and ate some ears of grain, rubbing them in their hands. But some of the Pharisees said, 'Why are you doing what is not lawful to do on the sabbath?' " They were objecting to a piece of technical sabbath breaking. Jesus had fallen foul of religious conservatism, the attitude which says, "We can't possibly do this or that because we have never done it before."

Jesus took the objection very seriously. He takes us all seriously whether we deserve it or not. "Jesus answered, 'Have you not read what David did when he was hungry, he and those who were with him: how he entered the house of God, and took and ate the bread of the Presence, which it is not lawful for any but the priests to eat, and also gave it to those with him?' And he said to them, 'The Son of man is lord of the sabbath.' "

He was saying two things here. First, there have always been changes, even in King David's day. Second, the basic principle for keeping the sabbath is not that of religious conservatism but the lordship of the Son of man, and by the Son of man Jesus meant himself! What a claim: "I am lord of the sabbath"! Only God incarnate could say such a thing. People had to make up their minds about him. What was he? Was he a blasphemous megalomaniac? Or was it conceivable that his authority was genuine and that actual Godhead was to be discerned in him? That is the great question which hovers over the pages of the Gospels. It is a crucial question which still confronts the world today.

Luke's narrative continues with another story in which the observation of the sabbath is an ingredient. "On another sabbath, when he entered the synagogue and taught, a man was there whose right hand was withered. And the scribes and the Pharisees watched him, to see whether he would heal on the sabbath, so that they might find an accusation against him." What a state of mind! They did not seem to care about the man with the crippled hand, but as we see from so many parts of the world today it is so easy for bigotry to drive out both compassion and common sense.

"But he knew their thoughts,"—better than they did— "and he said to the man who had the withered hand, 'Come and stand here.' " The standing up and coming forward were not without significance. In our healing services there is twofold symbolism. The coming forward symbolizes our availability to Jesus, the laying on of hands symbolizes his availability to us. So in the Gospel story the crippled man "rose and stood there." And Jesus said to the Pharisees, "I ask you, is it lawful on the sabbath to do good or to do harm, to save life or to destroy it?" Jesus was still striving to reach out and communicate with them. He knew that there were two types of cripple present, the man who was crippled by a maimed hand and the Pharisees who were crippled by prejudice. He wanted healing for all, but on this occasion he had to be satisfied with a single physical healing. There was sullen silence from the lawyers and Pharisees and so when Jesus had "looked around on them all, and said to him, 'Stretch out your hand.' And he did so, and his hand was restored."

It appears to have been an instantaneous healing. We see it happen in that way sometimes at our own services. I think of Janice, who had suffered from arthritis of the neck and head for years, till instantaneously at one of our services the pain vanished and has not recurred since; or Freda, who could not raise one of her arms above her shoulder before one of our services, but could wave it above her head afterward; or Samantha, whose leg was numb following an operation, till feeling returned during one of our services.

But these are exceptions. More often the healing reported to us is a more gradual process. Still, perhaps greater faithfulness and obedience to Jesus on our part would lead to a greater number of instantaneous healings. The implication of Scripture is certainly that in the presence of Christ healing could happen very quickly indeed.

The story has a sad ending. The lawyers and Pharisees "were filled with fury and discussed with one another what they might do to Jesus." We do not remain static after an encounter with Jesus. We find ourselves moving one way or another, toward him or away from him. The Jewish lawyers and ecclesiastics moved further and further away from him, and their hostility steadily increased, till they were obsessed with plots for his murder. Yet such is the wisdom of God that he used even that murder—in fact, supremely that murder—for the healing of the souls of men.

However, that murder was still some distance away. In the meantime Jesus had much to do—much healing, much teaching and much praying. We sometimes forget the importance to Jesus of prayer, but Luke was well aware of its centrality in his life and ministry. Following his encounter with the Pharisees we are told that he "went out into the hills to pray; and all night he continued in prayer to God." Then equipped and strengthened by prayer, he made what was to be a crucial decision. "And when it was day, he called his disciples, and chose from them twelve, whom he named apostles; Simon, whom he named Peter, and Andrew his brother, and James and John, and Philip, and Bartholomew, and Matthew, and Thomas, and James the son of Alphaeus, and Simon who was called the Zealot, and Judas the son of James, and Judas Iscariot, who became a traitor."

What an odd assortment! If we had been commissioned to choose twelve men whose leadership, wisdom and courage was to be a fundamental ingredient in God's plan to save the world, we would never have made a choice like this. They were not a particularly well-educated group. The first four were fishermen. They did not form a natural circle of friends. Matthew had collected taxes for the Romans and so would be regarded as a natural enemy by Simon, the freedom fighter, who had sworn to kill all who cooperated with Rome! They proved far from infallible. Peter denied Jesus. Thomas doubted Jesus. Judas betrayed Jesus.

So what was Jesus doing? He was doing what God always does. He was using the material at hand. He was refusing to force or manipulate human freedom. No doubt it would have been useful to have the high priest among the apostles and the Roman governor too. But the high priest and the Roman governor were not available. Not many "were wise according to worldly standards, not many were powerful, not many were of noble birth" who were committed to the Carpenter of Nazareth. So "God chose what is foolish in the world to shame the wise, God chose what is weak in the world to shame the strong" (1 Cor. 1:26-27). And he saw potential in those he called which nobody else would have dreamed.

It is very consoling when you and I consider our local church. What if the smart set of the neighborhood stay away? What if there is a dearth of rich or influential members? What if it is not a fashionable or culturally desirable parish? What if the people who do come to church are ill-assorted and nondescript? Then our situation is just about on the level with that of Jesus!

See what he did with his unlikely group. He had a two-stage plan. In Mark's account of the call of the Twelve he spells the plan out for us. Jesus ordained the Twelve first *"to be with him"* and then *"to be sent out"* (Mk. 3:14). Do we see these two elements in our own lives? Do we take time simply to be with Jesus? Are we conscious of his promise "where two or three are gathered in my name, there am I in the midst of them"? Do we keep stillness in his presence —not an empty stillness but a stillness of awareness, receptiveness and obedience? And when he sends us out, then are we ready to go?

This is all highly relevant to Christian healing. To be available to Christ's presence is to learn of his healing purposes and to receive his healing touch; to be sent out by him is to take that same healing influence into the world. It is no accident that the first thing which happened to the Twelve after their ordination was that Jesus "came down with them and stood on a level place, with a great crowd of his disciples and a great multitude of people from all Judea and Jerusalem and the seacoast of Tyre and Sidon, who came to hear him and to be healed of their diseases;

and those who were troubled with unclean spirits were cured. And all the crowd sought to touch him, for power came forth from him and healed them all" (Lk. 6:17-19).

And there we leave him. Or, rather, we do no such thing! I am writing these words on an Easter Monday. Yesterday I was reminding my congregation that Christian worship is not just a commemoration of a dead hero, it is a meeting with a risen living Lord and Savior, who with our consent will make all the difference in the world to us—and through us to the world. He is the same yesterday, today and for ever. He stands before us with the same loving gaze. He stands before us radiating the same healing power. He stands before us with the same authority and intent to cast out any evil which mars us. He offers the same commission: "Be with me. Then go for me. Let my healing hands be upon you. Then be my healing hands in the world!"

May I conclude this chapter by offering you another simple method of healing prayer? It is based on the practice of the presence of the living Christ.

1. Remember that Jesus is with you. "Lo, I am with you always, to the close of the age." He looks at you and you look at him. His gaze is full of love for you—not sentimental, indulgent love but realistic, costly, saving love, of the sort that we shall think about in the next chapter.

2. That love is radiant and vibrant with God's own healing and re-creating power. Picture and feel his hands upon you. Know that his will is for your wholeness.

3. Now he looks straight into you. He sees clearly all that spoils and hurts you, any sin, any negativity, any evil or alien element. He rebukes it with God's own authority, and says, "Come out of him," "Come out of her." Let Christ have his way. Try not to resist. He only casts out that which is harmful or worthless. Do not protect it against him. The forces of evil must retreat before him unless we give them sanctuary.

4. Now his hands are on you for healing again, because maybe the ministry of deliverance was painful for you. Let

his love and joy and peace flow about you and into you, stirring God's own life in your body, mind and spirit.

5. Now bring into his healing presence any for whom you wish to pray. You do not have to do anything. Just stand by, as Jesus looks at your friend, your neighbor, your loved one. Quietly and confidently align your will with that of his, as he speaks and touches the one for whom you are praying.

6. Finally his eyes and his hands are back upon you. It is his will to send you into the world on his behalf. He has something for you to do and to be and his hands are upon you for commissioning, for empowering, for the gift of the Holy Spirit so that you may have whatever resources are needful.

Go in peace and serve the Lord. In the name of Christ. Amen.

14/"By His Wounds We Are Healed"

There are two principal ways of coming into a ministry of Christian healing. There are those who become aware that they have a gift of healing and resolve that they must offer it to the Lord. On the other hand there are others who have no sort of awareness of a gift of healing but who embark upon this ministry in simple obedience to our Lord's command that his church should exercise a healing ministry just as he did himself (Lk. 9:1-2, 6; Lk. 10:1-9). Any necessary "gifts" they leave to the Lord's own provision.

I have come into the ministry of healing in this latter way and am grateful that it has been so for two reasons. First, the fact that I am not aware of any special personal gift of healing means that anyone who believes in the power of Jesus to bring wholeness to our sick world can do whatever I can do. If I had some strange and remarkable psychic force flowing through me, it might be very impressive, but Mr. and Mrs. Average Believer would have difficulty in identifying themselves with me. It is precisely because I am an ordinary vicar of an ordinary church with no awareness of extraordinary gifts or talents in the ministry of healing that I know I can invite *you* to share in this ministry.

Second, if I had some psychic gift to offer to the Lord, I might sometimes be tempted to rely on *it* rather than on *him*, whereas the essence of Christian healing whether or not the ministrant is aware of a personal gift must lie in a living encounter with the living Christ. I always dislike it if anyone refers to me as a "healer," because in the way in which I see Christian healing there is only one healer, and that healer is Jesus.

This surely is how it must be, because Christian healing is concerned not merely with physical cures but with wholeness of the entire person or, in other words, with salvation. Salvation and healing are inseparably interrelated. So if the gospel of salvation is being truly communicated, we should expect to see in the lives of those who receive it a movement toward wholeness of body, mind and spirit. When the saving power of Jesus was doubted, it was natural for him to say, "But look around you at the evidence. The blind receive their sight. The lame walk. The lepers are cleansed. The deaf hear. The dead are raised up!" (Mt. 11:4-5). On the other hand we should expect equally that any true ministry of Christian healing will involve the communication of the simplicities of the gospel. The two concepts are as inseparable as two sides of a coin. If anyone claims to practice Christian healing but does not overtly point to the saving power of Jesus Christ, his ministry is at best partial and at worst false.

If this is true, it has many implications. Above all it brings us to consider an element in Christian healing which is absolutely unique and which clearly distinguishes "Christian" healing from any other sort of healing. The supreme paradox and the supreme mystery of the Christian faith is that it is only as Jesus *dies* upon the cross that he saves us. So if saving and healing are inseparable, it is as Jesus *dies* upon the cross that he heals us. In the mysterious words of the book of Isaiah, "by his wounds we are healed."

But how can this be? How can the bleeding hand of Christ restore health to us? How can his dying breath be our breath of life?

These are deep issues—perhaps too deep for us to fathom adequately on this side of eternity. I hope that in attempting an answer I can avoid being glib, or superficial, or hiding behind religious jargon. Perhaps ordinary human relationships provide the best clues in a search for understanding, and perhaps the concept of forgiveness provides the best starting point.

It is not hard to see that forgiveness is a basic ingredient in the ministry of Christian healing. Mark 2:1-12 provides a good illustration. A paralyzed man was brought to Jesus on a stretcher by four friends. It was no easy task for them because Jesus was in a house packed with people and access to him was blocked by the crowd, but the four friends were determined and resourceful enough to make a hole in the roof and lower the stretcher down in front of Jesus. Their resourcefulness was rewarded.

Jesus healed the paralyzed man in two stages. The second stage was a simple command to take up his bed and walk, but before that something else had to be said and done. *Physical* liberation had to be preceded by *spiritual* liberation, and Jesus sensed that this was so. He sensed that there was a crippling burden of guilt which had to be removed before the body could be released from its paralysis, and so with all the authority which his oneness with the Father gave him he said, "My son, your sins are forgiven" (Mk. 2:5). And we are told that the paralyzed man stood up, picked up his stretcher and went out in the full and astonished view of the whole crowd.

In a similar way, sometimes I find that an assurance of forgiveness is an essential prerequisite of a physical healing. Joyce comes to mind, who came to see me because she suffered from a painful condition of the neck which meant that she had to wear a surgical collar. It eventually emerged that she also suffered from a severe burden of guilt in connection with a sin she had committed many years ago. She told me that every night before she went to sleep she asked the Lord over and over again to forgive her. I was able to share the Christian gospel of forgiveness with her and to suggest a change in her prayers. "Ask for forgiveness just once more," I suggested. "Ask for it simply and trustingly in the name of Jesus, who died on the cross to bring the forgiveness of God to us. Then know that God's forgiveness is yours. You don't have to ask for it anymore. Instead of saying, 'Lord forgive me,' say each night, 'Thank you, Lord, for forgiving me!'" So Joyce changed her way of thinking and of praying, and not only did her sense of guilt leave her but her neck pains went with it, and soon she was able to discard her surgical collar.

In both of these stories the offer of God's forgiveness constituted an explicit element in the ministry of Christian healing. Elsewhere, though it is not explicit, it is certainly implicit—just as I believe it is implicit in every facet of Christian life and ministry.

But what is forgiveness? And how does the death of Jesus bring it to us? Forgiving does not mean forgetting; it means remembering but going on loving just the same. It does not mean ignoring what has been done or putting a false label on an evil act; it means keeping your eyes wide open and yet being prepared to pay the price of maintaining a loving relationship. Even in human terms what a price this can be!

I think of Grace, a lovely Christian woman, whose husband has for some years been unfaithful to her and is not above treating her with physical violence. She sees precisely what sort of man he is but incredibly she goes on offering him her love. If he were to respond to that love it could make him a new man. Perhaps one day he will come to his senses, but in the meantime Grace goes on loving and forgiving and paying the cost.

I believe God treats people in a similar way. When God came in Jesus to our confused and fallen world, he came to offer us a relationship with him within which we might recover our senses and our wholeness. Grace can give some slight inkling of the costliness of this offer. It has involved God in loving and forgiving and paying the price of doing so on behalf of the whole human race. And what a price our sins exacted! The price proved to be no less than Christ's own lifeblood poured out upon the cross, not just as a tragic miscarriage of justice but as a deliberate sacrificial offering made for the love of you and me.

The cross is a place of pain, but also a place of triumph. Without it there could be no salvation for us. This is why we call the evil day on which human sin did its worst to Jesus *Good* Friday. It was good because on that day Love was true to itself and to us. Love neither compromised nor retreated before the evil and sickness and destructiveness in us. If it had compromised, it would have ceased to be Love and would have been irrelevant to our salvation. If it had turned its back and fled it would have ceased to be Love and again would have been irrelevant to us. But Jesus did neither. He stayed the course. He paid the price.

Because of Jesus and the price he has paid I can enter into a saving and healing relationship with God. I can come to God as my real and honest self, not pretending to virtue and wholeness which is not mine, but "just as I am." The evil and sickness and destructiveness which is in me will cause him the pain of death, but he takes the pain and death that I cause him and then rises again, still offering me the living, loving relationship within which I can recover the wholeness for which he made me.

It makes such a difference to know this. I think of Greg

whose story was told in detail in chapter eleven. Greg had a hard life and was heavy and sick with the anger he had swallowed back. His suppressed anger gave him all sorts of physical symptoms—headaches, nasal congestion, chest and heart pains, insomnia and with them a black suicidal depression. Underneath it all was smoldering murderous rage against the universe and the God who created it. It was an incredible liberation for Greg when he learned at the cross that God would accept him as he was, that he did not have to hold back and conceal the anger that was consuming him, that the real Greg could meet the real God, could ram on the crown of thorns, smash in the nails, and that the love of God would pay the price, die at his hands and rise again, still offering a relationship within which Greg's own wholeness could be rediscovered and re-created. It was lovely to see Christian healing come to Greg's body, mind and spirit as he encountered Christ on the cross.

Only Love which is prepared to die can enable us to relate to God just as we are, without pretense or self-deception, and only if we come before him as we really are can our healing in depth begin.

There are other factors too which we can discern in the healing power of the suffering and death of Jesus. For instance, some time ago I talked with a man who had been a prisoner of war in World War 2. He told me of the help that he had received from the chaplain in the prisoner-of-war camp, a chaplain for whom he had tremendous admiration because he had turned down an offer of repatriation just in order to stay with the men he felt called to serve. By contrast I remember being told with some scorn about a certain clergyman who visited a parishioner dangerously ill with an infectious disease. He stood at the bottom of the stairs and shouted up, "Woman, have you made your peace with God?"

The effectiveness of the prisoner-of-war chaplain and the ineffectiveness of the parson at the bottom of the stairs suggest a further line of thought as we seek to understand the healing power of the cross. It seems that if we really want to help each other we must be prepared to put ourselves side by side with those in trouble. The prophet Ezekiel put it in a nutshell when he wrote, "I sat where they sat" (Ezek. 3:15 KJV). Jesus did just that when, in a world where life is so often painful and bewildering, he did not flinch from sharing and identifying himself with man's pain and bewilderment.

I think of Ellen who was a mass of insecurity and anxiety. Her spirit was cringing with feelings of dread and dereliction which showed themselves in all kinds of strange illogical fears. If God was to reach her for healing he had to come to the place where she was. Somehow God had to feel God-forsaken if he was to share and infiltrate her situation. For Ellen healing began as she met the crucified Christ who cried, "My God, my God, why hast thou forsaken me?" It is the healing work of the crucified Christ to be sharing the suffering we endure as well as taking the consequences of the suffering we cause.

Of course, Jesus deserved none of it. His death was not for his deserts. It was for our sins and for our sake and for our healing. That was how much he loved us. That was how much he had to love us, if we were to be reconciled with God. The Scriptures say it all. "God was in Christ reconciling the world to himself, not counting their trespasses against them" (2 Cor. 5:19). "He himself bore our sins in his body on the tree, that we might die to sin and live to righteousness" (1 Pet. 2:24). "He was wounded for our sins, he was crushed for our wrong doing, the blows that fell upon him were for our peace, and by his wounds we are healed" (Is. 53:5).

Will you join me in this prayer?

"Lord God, I know that this is a sick world and that my sins are part of the sickness. I also know that, though I do not deserve it, Jesus, your son, has died for my healing. Through the crucified and risen love of Jesus, I am able to come to you, Father, and to find in you forgiveness, and peace, and eternal life. Stir in me the healing power of the Holy Spirit, both for my own wholeness and so that I may myself be a channel of healing in the world, in the name of Jesus. Amen."

15/Death

Greta was in the final stages of cancer. A colostomy had given her a few months of extra life, but it was a dubious mercy. Her body was wasted and ulcerous. She was never free from pain. And, as if this were not enough, her mental suffering matched the physical pain. Tension was written all over her face. She could not relax nor let her relatives relax. Though life was unbearable, the prospect of death was even more so. Nobody dared to mention it, even as a possibility.

One of the family asked me to call, and I visited Greta twice during the last fortnight of her life. We talked a little about her life, her home, her family—and then I broached the forbidden subject. "One of these days we're all going to die," I said. "Normally we don't think about it all that much, but I suppose a serious illness like this makes you start to think about it and to wonder about it."

To begin with she denied it, but I went on as gently as I could, "Well, you may find that the moment comes. In my job I have to think about it a great deal. I don't have any choice. The thing which makes it bearable is knowing that Christ is not only with me in life but he will be with me in death and he can cope with both." Gradually we began to talk about Jesus as the Lord of life and Conqueror of death. We spoke of his saving and healing work in life and in death. We prayed together, and I administered a laying on of hands in the name of Christ.

When I saw her a week later she had changed. She said that the pain was less severe and that her ulcer did not need to be dressed as often, but the most noticeable thing was that the tension had gone from her face. She was learning to rest in the presence of God, to trust him, to leave the issue of life and death in his hands. She had asked for a Bible and now read it every day. Her family noticed the difference in many ways. They were now allowed to sleep through the night without being continually called to see to her wants. The atmosphere was no longer brittle and forced. I actually enjoyed my last hour with Greta. She died a few days later.

There is such a thing as a "healed death." It is a privilege to witness it and to share the insights which it brings. It can have dignity and even beauty. It can reach out and touch the lives of those around, who paradoxically in the observation of death can begin to experience the stirrings of new dimensions of life.

I think of Dora, a deeply committed Christian woman, who developed a cancer which distorted her body and caused her terrible pain. Week after week I visited her. We talked together and prayed together. I laid hands on her and longed for her healing, but though she told me that the laying on of hands often brought a period of freedom from pain, physical healing did not follow. Her courage and her faith were undying but her body was not.

Her death saddened the whole church, the whole neighborhood. Why did she die? Why was there no physical healing after regular prayer and regular laying on of hands? I wish I knew. However, the situation was not without healing. I could feel the power of her love and her faith and so could others. After her death her husband, son and daughter-in-law began to come to church week after week. They came with inquiring minds and a readiness to learn. Dora had longed for it for years before her death, but it was only in and through her death that it began to happen.

It must infuriate Satan when death itself is used as a weapon against him! It happened supremely, of course, in the death of Jesus. It happened when early Christians chose to die in the Roman arenas rather than betray their Lord and their faith. Martyrdoms throughout the centuries have released the power of God, and at an ordinary domestic level whenever a Dora or a Greta offers death trustingly to the Lord, God's healing grace is enabled to flow.

Now a word about funerals. Every year the church is immensely privileged to have the opportunity to minister to millions of families going through times of bereavement and mourning. It may no longer be as common as it used to be to send for a clergyman in cases of impending death, but it is still normal practice to invite a clergyman to conduct a service after a death. This is a tremendous opportunity. I have no doubts whatsoever that every funeral service is a potential service of Christian healing and should be regarded as such. The fact that it is not usual to think of a funeral service in this way is, I believe, the greatest single missed opportunity in the church today.

Think for a moment of the situation at a typical funeral. For a time, even if a restricted time, there is a genuine openness to the challenge of spiritual reality. There are real hurts to be healed, real doubts to be faced, real questions to be answered. People come to the service wondering whether the Christian faith really can make a difference to

life and death or whether the whole funeral will be mean-
ingless. They come with a mixture of pain and guilt, anger,
anxiety and confusion and, for a time, there is a readiness
to receive spiritual truth. They wonder whether there is
such a thing as life after death and whether the story of the
resurrection of Jesus is fact or fairy tale. They wonder
whether there is a heaven and a hell.

Some contemplate not only the death of a loved one but
their own future death and their own present way of life.
Many are conscious of a sense of need, perhaps for the first
time in years. Some wonder whether the pastor really
believes the words of the service or whether he is just
going through the motions. If he has anything in his own
heart which can genuinely minister to the situation, they
want to know it and to test it. They often go away dis-
appointed after complete failure of communication, complete failure of healing.

I can remember clearly the two worst funerals I ever
attended. One was sentimental and maudlin. The prayer
was full of negative, unhelpful emotionalism. "Be with
your servant, Lord, when she returns to an empty house,
when she looks at the empty chair in which her loved
one will never sit again, when she sees the empty slippers
which he will never wear again.... " Almost sadistic!
Then there was the "tribute," which also served to em-
phasize the sense of loss. The other funeral was cold and
formal. The pastor rattled through the prayers in a remote,
impersonal voice. There was not even a handshake afterward.

I have heard both types of funeral defended, the former
on the grounds that people like a bit of emotion and expect to hear a recital of the virtues of the deceased; the
latter on the grounds that bereavement is a very painful,
personal time and that it is an impertinence to intrude
upon the privacy of the grief of those who mourn. However, the fundamental criticism of both types of service
must be that healing is unlikely to take place at either,

because on neither occasion is Christ likely to be made real to the people.

May I suggest that those of us who conduct funerals should *always* speak simply and directly of the faith which is in us? I am not for a moment saying that this is a time for manipulating the grief and weakness of mourners in order to engineer some sort of emotional response to an evangelistic appeal. That would be unpardonable. What I am pleading for is that, having thought and prayed about a funeral, we then look the mourners in the face, sense the nature of their needs, which will never be identical in the case of any two groups of mourners, and speak simply to those needs in the name and resources of the risen Christ. If he is a healing reality in our lives, if he is making a fundamental difference to our personal experience of life and our personal attitude to death, the mourners with their momentarily sharpened sensitivity will recognize spiritual truth for what it is. Lives can, and will, be touched and changed.

Several regular members of my own congregation started to come to church and to enter into a meaningful Christian experience because they first felt Christ's healing touch at a funeral service. It is a wonderful thing when a service instigated by death becomes an agency of healing and life. To see the burden lift from the face of a mourner because one has spoken Christ's healing word is one of the supreme joys of the ministry. And it is a paradoxical and marvelous thing to see new life begin at a funeral.

16/Distant Healing

Some people who have no objection to the concept of a direct person-to-person ministry of Christian healing balk at the idea of distant healing or the idea that one can receive a laying on of hands by proxy for someone else who may be many miles away. I know of a doctor who sat uneasily through a church council meeting while Christian healing was being discussed, but stood up and walked out in protest as soon as mention was made of distant healing. He felt that the discussion had moved into the realm of superstition and mumbo jumbo.

But Jesus certainly exercised distant healing. He did not minister directly to the centurion's servant. The centurion did not expect him to do so. "Just give the order," he said, "and my servant will get well" (Lk. 7:7 TEV), and that was the way it happened.

It still happens that way. One Christmas Eve my wife went into church and found a parishioner, a former head nurse, praying there. She was in a state of considerable distress because her teen-age son had had an operation and had been sent home from the hospital, but his condition had deteriorated. "I have seen patients die after operations," she said. "I can recognize the signs and I am afraid for my son." I telephoned her later, after my wife had told me the story. We were due to celebrate our Christmas Eve Midnight Communion. I told her that if she wished it we would pause in the middle of the service and the whole congregation would pray for her son. She gratefully accepted.

Later she told me that as we prayed for him in church his restlessness settled, he fell into a deep sleep, and the next day he was very much better and clearly on the way to recovery. A coincidence? If so, there are more of them.

The vicarage telephone rang one day during a week following one of our services of "Rediscovery of Christian Healing." My wife answered it and a woman's voice said, "You don't know me, but I feel I must call to say thank you for Sunday's service. I came to it because I was at my wits' end. My son is seriously ill mentally. He has been receiving psychiatric treatment in and out of the hospital for many months, and recently he has been worse than ever. I heard about your service and came to receive a laying on of hands by proxy on his behalf. I want you to know that since then his condition has improved out of recognition. For the first time in months, I can see light and hope in the situation."

Another coincidence? Then how about this? One of our congregation was worried about a relative in the south of England who had gone into the hospital for an operation, and so she received a laying on of hands by proxy for her. Later her relative told her, "I was very upset and agitated when I went into the hospital but while your service was taking place something strange happened to me. I experienced a great feeling of calm, which persisted afterward. I had an excellent night and next day awoke without feelings of anxiety. I felt able to trust myself to the surgeons without fear and the operation was a complete success." A third coincidence? One is reminded of the words of William Temple: "I find that when I pray coincidences happen. When I cease to pray, coincidences stop happening."

Another person in the south of England was healed of diabetes insipidus at the same time that one of our congregation was receiving a proxy laying on of hands on her behalf. Paradoxically, the member of St. George's who received the proxy laying on of hands herself suffered from sugar diabetes but this condition was untouched.

Perhaps I may add one further story of distant healing, a rather personal one. A few years ago I was saddened to receive a letter from my mother, who at that time lived in Cornwall. In it she told me that she was not well. She normally writes happy letters, but the tone of this one was thoroughly depressed. For weeks she had been suffering from a twofold condition in which painful sciatica was combined with a rash of ugly, irritating pustules, which resisted all attempts at treatment. As I read the letter my first reaction was to feel completely helpless, over 350 miles away from her, but I went into my study and there quietly sought to convey some sort of distant healing to her in the name of Christ. Her next letter was an amazing transformation. The sciatica and the rash had both cleared up. "The sky is blue and life is good," she wrote.

There the story might have ended, another possible coincidence to add to the list. But some weeks later, in a further letter, she felt she must tell me the details of her experience of healing. After beginning, "I hope you won't feel I am going off my head," she went on to say how (at about the same time at which, unknown to her, I was endeavoring to channel Christ's healing power to her) she felt moved to go to her bedroom. There on an impulse she touched the palm cross which I had sent her from St. George's. Immediately in her mind's eye she was kneeling at the communion rail at St. George's and was receiving a laying on of hands. This was administered by two people, one of whom she recognized as me, the other she felt was George Bennett, although she had never met him or seen his photograph. A sense of peace came over her and immediately her condition began to improve.

Some days later she was watching television and a picture of George Bennett appeared on the screen as part of an advertisement for the forthcoming program on Christian healing from St. George's Church. The face was exactly the face she had seen in the mental picture she had received in her bedroom days before. It would really take a piece of mental gymnastics to attribute that to coincidence!

So in my own limited experience there are occasions on which Christian healing has taken place over a distance and without a person-to-person encounter. Others who undertake a ministry of healing tell me that the same is true also in their experience.

On reflection I cannot see that there is any reason to think distant healing a strange thing if we believe in prayer. The doctor who walked out of his church council when distant healing was mentioned must have prayed for people who were some distance from him. It is a commonplace of prayer to ask God's protection for and blessing upon absent friends and loved ones. God is everywhere and therefore he is a bridge in time and space between us and our loved ones. To receive a laying on of hands by proxy is an acted prayer, and if any power at all is released by prayer there is no logical reason why it should not be released by the ministry of distant healing.

17/The God Within

"**I** believe in the Holy Spirit." I say so every Sunday, and so does my congregation. But I wonder how many of us have really paused to work out the enormity of the doctrine we are professing and of the claim we are making?

If you and I are prepared to say that we believe in the Holy Spirit, the third person of the Holy Trinity, we are saying that we do not just believe in the Creator God who is the ground and source of all creation, known and unknown. We do not just believe that in a remarkable way God's true nature has been revealed to us in the life and death and essence of our Savior Jesus Christ. We are also saying that we believe in our own capacity for oneness with the Godhead.

The devil is always telling us that the Christian faith has a low doctrine of self. "Come to me," he says, "and I will give you a proper sense of your own importance. Stay away from Jesus or he'll have you groveling in no time, because to be a Christian is to be self-depreciatory and self-contemptuous."

The truth is in fact the very opposite. If you are interested in the lowest possible concept of the value of man, then go to the devil! While it is true that the devil encourages self-centeredness, the self-centeredness he most favors is a strange mixture of self-conceit and self-contempt. It is miles away from genuine self-respect. Often it cannot bear to look at itself honestly and survives only by pretense and self-delusion. And the devil is not called "the destroyer" for nothing. The paths of sin are the paths of self-destruction. Think of a sin—hate, lust, greed, jealousy, any sin at all. Do not attitudes like these self-evidently diminish the human spirit and in the last resort threaten to destroy it?

By contrast, if it is a high concept of man you are after, try the gospel. True, the gospel tells me I need to be cleansed from my sins, but this is not because I am worthless, it is because I am too precious to stay uncleansed. If I wash my body when it becomes dirty, it is not because my body is unimportant to me but because I think it worth caring for. If when I sustain a physical injury or sickness, I send for a doctor, it is because my body is too important for me to allow sickness to go untreated. Similarly the concern of the Christian gospel that Christ should minister to the sickness of my soul is a sign of the value that my Father puts upon me.

God made each one of us in his own image. Each one of us constitutes a walking miracle just by existing, and as for our ultimate potential, words cannot express it. We have marred this image by our sin and stupidity, but God is not defeated. We have a Savior. By crib and cross God has shared our nature that we might share his. And from the Father and the Son proceeds the Holy Spirit, the God within, by whom and for whom we were made, the God who stands at the root of our deepest nature and affirms our truest self.

What difference does it make if we really believe in the God within? It makes, quite literally, all the difference in the world. The concept of the God within is not just a doctrine but the basis for a host of practicalities, as is always the case with Christian theology.

Consider, for instance, the implication of this concept for Christian conduct. It must make a difference to my dealing with my neighbors if I have some hint of their potential as persons redeemed and transformed by the Holy Spirit.

Consider too its implication for those occasions when we are targets for some sort of temptation. Satan's blandishments must surely seem less attractive if we have a firm grasp upon the Christian concept of selfhood. Think of yourself—created as you are in God's image, loved all the way to the cross by Jesus, and designed to be one with God's own Holy Spirit. There is no improving on that for destiny. To hang the devil's tawdry trappings about such a creature would be as senseless as taking a necklace of priceless pearl and spraying it with cheap gaudy paint!

And of course true belief in the Holy Spirit must logically have the most profound effect on our approach to Christian healing. If my own deep nature is being transformed from one degree of glory to another by the God within, then ailments of body, mind and spirit are out of place and can have no more than a passing foothold. To stir the Spirit in ourselves and in others must be a powerful act of healing.

So may I offer you a further method of healing prayer? We have already thought of a method of healing prayer based on an awareness of the peace of God the Father and a second method based on the practice of the presence of God the Son, our Lord Jesus Christ. Here now is a meditation on the healing work of God the Holy Spirit.

1. Recollect the promise of Jesus: Your heavenly Father *will* give the Holy Spirit to those who ask him (Lk. 11:13).

2. All who put their faith in Jesus as Lord and Savior may and should claim this promise. Otherwise our Christianity will be tragically incomplete. The gift of the Holy Spirit has been God's deep purpose for us since our creation. "God has shared our manhood that we might share his Godhead" (Athanasius). Jesus promised his disciples, "The Holy Spirit will be in you" (Jn. 14:17). Just as being a Christian involves taking God the Father on trust from Jesus, equally it involves taking on trust from him God the Holy Spirit. So here and now, simply and trustingly, claim the promise of the Holy Spirit. If in your own life you have decided Jesus is to be trusted then his promise of the Holy Spirit is also to be trusted. Claim the promise. Thank God for the fact of the Holy Spirit in *you*.

3. As with wonder you recollect the God within, remember that the Holy Spirit is the Lord and giver of life. Feel and enjoy the life of God surging in you. Make a mental act of assent and cooperation with the life of God in you—the life of God stirring in every cell of the body, the life of God sharpening and enlightening your mind, the life of God fitting your spirit for eternal life. The God within is at work to help you become your true self, the *you* that God envisaged since the beginning of time. Say yes to your true self.

4. The life of God in you stirs and moves with God's own strength and God's own goodness. Picture the life of God in you, gently but inevitably nudging aside all that is in you which is alien to your true self, all that hurts or spoils your body, mind or spirit. Relax and let the God within have his way with you.

5. The life of God within you is one with the ring of peace around you and the healing Lord who has introduced you to both Father and Spirit. Also the Holy Spirit in you is one with the Holy Spirit in those who are around you. Recollect Jesus' prayer to the Father for all believers: "that they may be one even as we are one, I in them and thou in me, that they may become perfectly one" (Jn. 17:22-23). Pray for the church of God, that it may be active

and alive by its oneness with the Holy Spirit. Picture your own church being led by the Holy Spirit into life and love and truth and healing power. Offer this mental picture to God in simple trust that it may be so in the Lord's name. Picture the life of God in every person for whom you feel called to pray. There is no person to whom the life of God is completely alien. Thank God that his life is good, and again in simple trust pray that God may have his own healing and saving way in all his creatures.

6. Finally wait upon the Holy Spirit in silence for some moments. The Father has something for you to do and to be. The Holy Spirit in you is one with the Father and knows his will for you. And with that knowledge he has the necessary gifts and resources for that will to be done through you. Be still and know the purpose and the power of the kingdom of God within you.

7. Then go in the power of that same Holy Spirit, who as the true God is at work to make you your true self. Touch the world for healing.

18/How Does Christian Healing Work?

Ｗe have looked at some of the reasons for believing in the reality and importance of Christian healing. We have looked at the breadth of its application and scope. It may now be helpful to ask how it actually works. What are its resources and its channels?

The resources which underlie Christian healing are threefold. There are the creative energies of God the Father which have been in the universe since its genesis and which are about and in us always. There are the saving mercies of God the Son, available to us through his life, death and resurrection. There is the life-giving power of God the Holy Spirit, available to all who make themselves available to him. We have already seen that there are many varied channels through which this healing can flow. Here now, listed for convenience, are nine of these channels of healing.

Perhaps the first to come to mind, though not, I think, the most important, is the laying on of hands in the name of Christ. Jesus himself laid hands on the sick. For instance, after the healing of Peter's mother-in-law: "Now when the sun was setting, all those who had any that were sick with various diseases brought them to him; and he laid his hands on every one of them and healed them" (Lk. 4:40). He promised that believers "will lay their hands on the sick, and they will recover" (Mk. 16:18). It is not just the clergy who may do this. It is a ministry given to the church as a whole.

This is why at St. George's and St. Stephen's we involved both clergy and laity in the laying on of hands at services. Of course it should not be confined to services. The touch of Christ can be conveyed on any occasion formally or informally. It is not even necessary to say, "I am going to administer a laying on of hands in the name of Christ." It can happen naturally on all sorts of occasions. I was out for a walk and happened to meet one of the men of the congregation who was off work with a bad back. I did not attempt to say what I was doing but as he told me where the pain was I touched each place with a silent prayer. Afterward he told me that he knew just what I was doing even though not a word was spoken. There was an immediate improvement in his condition and he was soon back at work.

If the touch is to be accompanied by an audible prayer, it must be a prayer which is right and natural for the ministrant. Jesus was able to say, "Take up your bed and walk!" I would suggest that few of us have the spiritual perception or the flow of healing to be able to say that, except perhaps under the strongest of impulsions from the Lord on a specific occasion.

But we may find words which are right for us at our particular level of spiritual development—perhaps as simple as, "God bless you," perhaps specifically introducing the thought of healing, "God bless you and heal you." In our

Christian healing services we say, "May the healing power of the Holy Spirit be in you," sometimes varying the words to match the church's year, saying for instance at Christmas, "May the healing power of the Christ Child work in you." Sometimes I adapt a blessing: "The Lord bless you and keep you, the Lord make the light of his face shine upon you and grant you healing and peace." Sometimes I weave a prayer around the threefold resources of Christian healing: "May the creative energies of the Father, and the saving mercies of Jesus Christ and the life-giving power of the Holy Spirit work in you and heal you from all that hurts you."

Prayer can be a channel of healing without a laying on of hands. This is true of both public and private prayer, prayer for others and prayer for ourselves. Personally I believe that a prayer for healing should never be accompanied by the words, "if it be thy will." But it is equally true that we should avoid a rigid state of mind. We may not know the nature of the healing which is most needed and our rigidity may itself be a block to healing.

The spoken word can be full of healing. "My son," says the book of Proverbs, "be attentive to my words; incline your ear to my sayings. Let them not escape from your sight; keep them within your heart. For they are life to him who finds them, and healing to all his flesh" (4:20-22). In the chapter on death I was pleading for "the healing word" to be an integral part of every funeral. People sometimes say afterward, "I do feel better. You have made such a difference to me." This is also the purpose of the expositon of Scripture at our Christian healing services.

If it can be a healing act to speak in the name of Christ, it can also be a healing act to listen in his name. It is often said that since we have two ears and one mouth we ought to do twice as much listening as talking. There is a great deal of truth and importance in this for those who would exercise a ministry of healing. An effective counseling session, despite its name, is mostly a matter of listening.

There would have been no healing for Greg and Betty and many of the other people mentioned in these pages if I had not been prepared to listen and to keep on listening. Often, oddly enough, when the healing word is spoken, it is spoken not by the counselor but by the person being counseled. That person has known it all along, but has needed to be heard out in order to come to the point of admitting it to himself or herself.

There is healing, too, in every good relationship. If a church is true to its calling to be the family of God, the day-to-day encounter of member with member in Christian fellowship will be rich in healing. One of our former curates has a teen-age son with Down's syndrome. From the start his parents have loved and accepted him and when he came to St. George's the congregation did the same. It was a moving experience to see him grow and blossom under that love. He is still a mongoloid but he has an infectious happiness and a lively independence, both of which are the product of real Christian healing.

As far as worship is concerned it would be wrong to think that healing is confined to services of Christian healing. If the church had not neglected Christian healing over the years, specific services of healing might not now be necessary. Healing would be a normal feature of services as a whole. We have already looked at funeral services as services of healing. Perhaps special mention should also be made of Holy Communion, the act of worship directly given to the church by Jesus. It is a normal part of every communion service to pray for the sick and claim Christ's power to heal, and the Anglican prayer book service makes it plain that the purpose of the giving of bread and wine to each communicant is so that the body and blood of Christ may "preserve thy body and soul to everlasting life." At St. George's it seemed natural to us to include at our midweek celebration of Holy Communion a list of the names of those sick people for whom we wished as a church to pray, and it was not uncommon to find a communicant with tears in his or her eyes—often a sign of the healing touch of Christ.

In this list of channels of Christian healing I ought, I think, to refer to the practice of unction. We are told in Mark 6:13 that the disciples of Jesus "anointed with oil many that were sick and healed them." James instructs Christian elders to anoint the sick with oil in the name of the Lord (Jas. 5:14). In the past I have taken it that these verses contained an instruction to provide simple medical care rather than to perform a symbolic act of healing. Certainly in the story of the Good Samaritan, oil was poured into the wounds of the man who fell among thieves for medical purposes and not as a spiritual symbol. Similarly Isaiah 1:6 speaks of wounds being softened with oil. However it is indisputable that many people find unction a powerful channel of Christian healing and I have now begun to incorporate it in my own ministry.

Ordinary medical care may itself, of course, be a channel of Christian healing and often is so. It adds a new dimension to medical care if it is regarded by both doctors and patients as an expression of the ministry of divine healing. I have the feeling, for instance, that a pill or a medicine may well be more effective if one asks God's blessing on it (perhaps in the form of a sort of "grace") before taking it.

This chapter is not an attempt to produce an extensive list of channels of Christian healing, but there is perhaps one further addition which should be made to it. I think of two teen-age girls—let's call them Franchette and Josephine—who came to the vicarage one day in a state of considerable agitation. They had become mixed up in a circle which dabbled in the occult. Franchette was now a very troubled person. She said that everywhere she went she was dogged by the sense of an evil presence. It was, she said, as though someone or something malevolent was continually walking behind her. The two girls had both withdrawn from any practices connected with the occult, but the feeling of an evil presence persisted. Skeptics might doubt its objective reality but no one could doubt the reality of the harm it was doing to Franchette. Josephine was almost equally worried as she could see the effect which all of this was having upon her friend.

We went into church. The girls knelt at the communion rail and I stood behind it. I gave Franchette a crucifix to hold to concentrate her thoughts and I prayed, not in any set form but as the words came, thanking God for his goodness and power, thanking him for making that goodness and power available to us in Jesus Christ. I praised God for the fact that Christ is stronger than any power of evil and that the strong, triumphant, risen Christ was present with us there and then. I claimed his power to banish whatever it was that was troubling Franchette and prayed that God's Holy Spirit might be in her to hallow and protect her life. Franchette knelt for a while and then stood and said, "It has gone. For the first time in weeks it isn't there anymore."

I suggested to her that she should now maintain a closeness to holy things and should worship regularly. She was from another neighborhood and had deliberately come to a church other than her own for help because she did not want the story known by her own friends and neighbors. So I would have had no means of knowing how she fared subsequently had not Josephine written to me some time later. She put no address at the top of the letter because she, like Franchette, wanted to remain as anonymous as possible, but she said that she felt she must write to say that Franchette was now completely normal again and that there had been no recurrence of the trouble. She wanted to say how grateful they both were and that they would never again dabble in the occult.

Some might give the rather grand name of exorcism to that incident. It illustrates the point that sometimes Christian healing is not just a matter of soothing a hurt but involves rebuking and driving out an evil. It may be an evil connected in some way with the occult. It may be a spirit of fear, or a spirit of lust, or some other aspect of evil. These things can have a stranglehold upon life but Christ can break that stranglehold. The casting out of evil goes hand in hand with healing in the Gospels and as the church begins to rediscover Christian healing it is important that we should also rediscover a realistic, sensible, scriptural ministry of deliverance from evil.

19/Who Needs Healing?

We all need healing. Sometimes we do not realize the exact nature of our need for healing. Sometimes we actively resist that knowledge.

Healing is like saving. We all need saving, but among men everywhere there is widespread resistance to the idea. It is easy to see that the villains of history were sinners—people like Nero or Hitler. But we are tempted to disassociate ourselves from folk like that. We say to ourselves, "I don't commit murder or rape my neighbor's wife or rob old ladies in the street or anything like that. I'm as good as the next man." The trouble is that he is a sinner too. We both need saving. Neither of us loves God with all our hearts. Neither of us loves our neighbors as we love ourselves. If either of us were to stand beside Jesus, the light of his goodness and love would reveal us as the sinners that we are. The first step toward letting Jesus do his saving work is to let him show us that we need it.

It is much the same with healing, as one would expect, since "healing" and "saving" often translate the same Greek word in the New Testament. I remember Herbert arguing about his own need for healing. He thought it a great idea that I should go around the parish administering a laying on of hands to people who were obviously sick, but he was adamant that he did not need it. He had a bit of a cold, he said, but that was all. Apart from that he was in perfect health. A year later he came to the communion rail at a service of healing for a laying on of hands. He had thought his way through it and now saw it very differently.

At a purely physical level we are rarely 100 per cent fit, at a mental level few of us could claim to be perfectly integrated persons, and at a spiritual level we all have temptation problems. Who would be rash enough to claim that all his or her relationships are completely healthy? Who would be stupid enough to say that we do not live in a sick society and who would be so conceited as to claim that he or she personally has absolutely no part in the sickness of that society? Perfect health in body, mind and spirit, in thought, word and deed—that is what we have to claim before the healing touch of Christ will be irrelevant to us. Herbert came to see that he could make no such claim. Now he receives the ministry of healing regularly, and it is beginning to change and heal him.

So who needs healing? We all do. I do. You do. With this in mind perhaps I may try to offer some practical thoughts to you and to myself with a view to our personal healing. If we are to experience the healing touch of Christ upon our lives in its fullness, it is important for us to cultivate a spirit of flexible availability. Rigidity is the enemy of healing.

There are two types of rigidity which commonly hinder healing. One is the rigidity of hopelessness. Every doctor knows how hard it is to bring healing to a patient who has decided his or her case is hopeless and has given up the will to live. The devil loves to stir up feelings of despair in us. "You'll never get better," or "You'll never cope with your feelings of fear. You'll always feel depressed, guilty, burdened. You'll never fight this or that temptation. You're hooked. You're an addict. Give up," says the devil. "Curse God and die."

But of course the devil is a liar. If we put ourselves and our trouble in the healing hand of God, if we rest and relax in his presence, if we trust his love and his wisdom, we shall find that God's healing power can and will infiltrate the situation, transforming it. There were dire predictions about the church warden whose story I told in chapter six. But they came to nothing.

As we saw in chapter eleven, Greg could see no way out of his depression. "You can't help me. Nobody can," he said. But Christ could and did. Even if a condition ends in death—and it will for all of us sooner or later—the experience of death can be transformed by the healing, triumphant power of the risen Christ, as it was in the case of Greta in chapter fifteen. So beware of the rigidity of hopelessness.

The second type of rigidity is perhaps more subtle. It places preconditions on the form which healing is to take. We saw in chapter six that in insomnia the more rigidly one concentrates on going to sleep, the more wakeful one is liable to become. Similarly, after an operation or after a dose of flu it is never a good thing to set oneself a rigid timetable for recovery. "On day one I shall feel in such a fashion and do this. On day two I shall feel a degree better and do that," and so on. It rarely works that way. There are good days and bad days. Rigidity of expectation can be a barrier to recovery. Turning this sort of rigidity into the form of a prayer barely disguises it. Christian healing means letting God have his way with us, not superimposing our will upon him!

One reason why it is wrong to be rigid is that God knows

the nature of the blocks to healing which have to be circumvented, whereas we may not. Another reason is that we may not know where our own deepest need for healing lies. We may be conscious of a physical condition but unaware that there is a more serious spiritual condition underlying it. God's concern is with the whole of us, not just with partial or symptomatic conditions.

A man phoned me to ask if I could make his bad back better. I explained that what I had to offer him was the fullness of the healing power of Jesus Christ and that Jesus was interested not just in his back but in the whole of him, body and soul, every part of his life. There was a pause and then he said, "That wasn't what I had in mind," and hung up. At any rate he saw the distinction and had a glimpse of what the church has to offer, even if he went on to reject it.

So if we wish to open ourselves to Christian healing the first step is to admit our need for healing and the second is to make ourselves available and flexible to the healing power of the Holy Spirit. We have to be prepared to pray, "Holy Spirit, come into me and have your healing way. Help me to see the things which you wish to show me. Help me to hear the things which you wish to tell me. Help me to receive the things which you wish to give me." If we pray in this way either for ourselves or for someone else, we must be prepared for the unexpected to happen.

I think of an accountant who attended a group to pray for the health of a sick friend and unmistakably received a call to the ministry while doing so. I think of the many occasions when God had used one of my own prayers for healing to show me an aspect of myself which I would have preferred not to see, some facet of myself needing the healing touch of Christ.

We should not worry if the first symptoms of Christian healing appear counterproductive. A continuing openness will often reveal a reason for it. Geraldine came to see me in a greatly upset state after receiving a laying on of hands. She had undergone an experience of severe panic shortly after the service and had to be put to bed, trembling. It emerged that she had brought a phobic condition to the service in the hope that it would be healed. Following the service the lost roots of her phobia had come back to consciousness. I was able to minister to them and to her in the name of Christ. She went on to begin to experience a new liberty.

New liberty is a characteristic of healed life in Christ. Jesus said, "If you continue in my word ... you will know the truth, and the truth will make you free. ... So if the Son makes you free, you will be free indeed" (Jn. 8:31, 32, 36). "Where the Spirit of the Lord is, there," says St. Paul, "is freedom" (2 Cor. 3:17).

A final thought about our own healing, our own liberation. Christian healing is not just a flash in the pan, a magic moment; it is a way of life, a lifelong process. Who needs healing? I do. And I shall need it tomorrow, and the day after, and the day after that. The complexities of healing match the complexities of my own body, mind and spirit; the complexities of my thoughts and words and deeds; the complexities of every relationship in my past, present and future. And it is never a static or self-restricted influence. When I receive freely, I am expected to give freely. Just as we are loved in order to love, and forgiven in order to forgive, so *we are healed in order to heal.*

20/Invitation to Christian Healing

If I have a vision for tomorrow's church, it is that it will receive God's healing power more deeply and channel it into the world more effectively. By the church I do not mean just "them"—the powers that be, the leaders in high places. Nor do I mean just "them"—the folk with magic in their hands because they have perhaps some special psychic gift for healing. I mean "us"—ordinary folk like me, and perhaps like you.

I hope that the pictures I have conveyed of St. George's, Hyde, and St. Stephen's, Prenton, are those of ordinary churches, churches with which anyone can easily identify. St. Paul speaks of "gifts of healing" in 1 Corinthians 12. Anyone having such a gift must praise God for it and use it in God's service. But if you do not feel that you have such a gift, take comfort. At St. George's and St. Stephen's our basic awareness has not so much been that of having any sort of special gift, but rather that of having a specific command from Christ. One of the church officers at St. George's used to feel that he might have a gift of healing, but there was no evidence that healing took place to a greater extent when he was involved in our laying on of hands service than when he was not. Similarly, when we had our Mission of Teaching and Healing most of the instances in which healing and blessing were reported involved a laying on of hands not by George Bennett but by the other clergy who assisted. Christ's command to the church is "heal." If we obey him, we may leave the provision of "gifts" in his hands.

There is considerable variety in the forms which a ministry of healing can take. Sometimes it can appear sensational, extraordinary, even bizarre. By contrast our ministry has been a quiet, unemotional and in many ways rather ordinary affair. Initially there was no publicity because we did not want it and because there really was not much to publicize. There was no outright hostility to this ministry in the church, perhaps because many of our congregation were not convinced that anything important was happening. Some still feel that way, although the consciousness of the centrality of Christian healing in the life and ministry of the church is steadily increasing. In one way I regret that I cannot write a more spectacular book, but in another way perhaps it is good that it should be so. Our very ordinariness is your comfort and your challenge. This book is a manual by a beginner for beginners. If Christian healing can come to St. George's and St. Stephen's, it can come anywhere!

So where do we go from here? I have tried to make this a practical book, so may I add a further practical suggestion? May I suggest that you collect a small group of fellow Christians and together go through the chapters of this book critically and in detail, one by one. Ask of each chapter the question, *"Is this true?"* You may care to apply five tests of the truth.

1. Is each chapter true to the teaching of the Bible *as a whole*, so far as you understand it?

2. Is it true to what you know of Christ?

3. Is it true to reason?—for God gave us minds and he means us to use them.

4. Is it true to experience, both personal experience and the experience of history, including the traditional experience of the church?

5. Is it true to the promptings of the Holy Spirit in you?

These are five tests which I regularly apply to new ideas and propositions. If an idea is false it founders on one or more of these tests, sometimes on all of them.

As far as the illustrative incidents and the case histories are concerned, the names are fictitious and one or two details have been changed, but basically they are true and as objective as I have been able to make them. Where possible I have avoided technical medical or psychiatric terminology, because it would seem wrong for me to set myself up as an amateur doctor or psychiatrist, although our spheres of concern overlap to some extent. I have also been on my guard against overstatement and wishful thinking. These stories can of course be paralleled and exceeded by stories in many other books about Christian healing. See, for instance, the two books by George Bennett, which were mentioned in chapter three.

If, after critical scrutiny, your group comes to the conclusion that this book is basically true, may I then suggest a second question: *"Is it important?"* Not all truth is equally important. The truth, for instance, about the mating habits of a wart hog might only be important to a zoologist or another wart hog! It would have a limited concern. Is Christian healing like that—interesting only to those who like that sort of thing? Or is it, as I have been suggesting, universal in its application and importance?

Here are some questions to help you decide. Do you believe Christ really did heal folk who were ill in body,

mind and spirit? Do you believe him when he says,
"Where two or three are gathered in my name, there am I
in the midst of them" (Mt. 18:20)? Do you believe that
Jesus has not changed—that he is the same yesterday,
today and tomorrow? Then it follows that the Christ in the
midst of Christians is a healing Christ today as ever and
that he still bids the church to be healed in order to heal.
Is that important? Does every single chapter in this book,
however inadequate and partial, point to something
central and urgent in God's call to the church?

The third question follows naturally. If there is both
truth and importance in the concept of Christian healing,
then *what are we going to do about it?* It was a question
I had to face for myself and still have to face. The effectiveness of today's church and tomorrow's church depends to a
large extent on our answer to that question. Is the church
prepared, are we prepared to be available to the healing
power of Christ? Will we admit our need, our sickness?
Will we admit his power? Will we hear his call to channel
his healing into this sick world at every level?

A year ago one of our neighboring parishes instituted
a midweek service of healing with the laying on of hands.
Some months ago the vicar told me this remarkable story.
A local couple who longed for a baby but had been child-
less for eight years asked for a service of healing to bring
God's power and love to the condition of childlessness.
The service was arranged, and it was agreed that it should
also be a proxy form of ministration and prayer for the
husband's father who was in the hospital with a cancer
condition in which a lung was collapsed. (There was also
a probability of secondary growths in the brain.) Husband
and wife received prayer, laying on of hands and anoint
ing. Very soon the wife learned she was pregnant and
within days of the service the father's lung reinflated and
an X ray could find no trace of any cancer whatsoever! My
colleague tells me he is conscious of no special gift of
healing. He says, "I just try to obey the gospel orders!"

There seems little doubt that a similar awareness of gospel orders is today leading more and more to an involvement in the ministry of Christian healing. Whether they are high, low or middle in their churchmanship seems not to matter. With increasing frequency letters come to me asking for prayer for this church or that because the members are just about to start services of healing. Of course there is more to the ministry of Christian healing than an occasional service and a periodic laying on of hands. Christian healing is a way of life, a way of love, a way of prayer, a way of expectant recognition that Jesus is the same yesterday, today and forever. There is so much to ponder, so far to go. But "a journey of a thousand miles begins with a single step." Whenever a group of Christians take that step, or when even a single individual does so, the kingdom of God comes a little nearer.

What then can you and I do to respond to Jesus' invitation to identify ourselves with him in his healing work? We can all undertake healing prayer of a sort similar to that described earlier in the book. If we incorporate it into our daily prayers, we shall inevitably be the better for it ourselves, and others, too, will feel the benefit.

However, perhaps you are in a position to do more than this. Perhaps you can bring the challenge of the ministry of healing to the notice of your local church. If so, why not? It is a comprehensive ministry, relevant to our wholeness at every level of body, mind and spirit, relevant to the problems and potential of neighborhoods and nations. It is a logical ministry—true to human reason, so far as reason goes, and rooted in much experience. It is a responsible ministry, for it takes the concept of the church as the body of Christ seriously and recognizes that his work must be our work. It is a scriptural ministry because a Bible from which all reference of healing had been expurgated would be no more than shreds and fragments. It is a ministry of exploration and rediscovery—much needed where the church is stagnant. It is a stretching and challenging ministry, much needed where the church is complacent. It is a ministry of close union with the Lord, much needed where the church is worldly. It is a ministry through which the power of God can be discerned and unleashed, but is nonetheless within the reach of ordinary Christians and ordinary churches.

It is not a heretical ministry because it does not spring from any novelty of doctrine but, as we have seen, it is firmly founded upon belief in God the Father, God the Son and God the Holy Spirit. It is not a presumptuous ministry because it makes us continually subordinate to the Lord's Word and dependent upon his saving power.

The invitation to Christian healing comes from no less a source than Jesus himself. It requires a response, like a card marked R.S.V.P. For centuries all too few have acknowledged this invitation, but it has never been withdrawn.

It comes to *you* now.